CRAFTING with FLOWERS

CRAFTING
with FLOWERS

Celebrate the Seasons
with 20 Floral Projects

Bex Partridge

Quadrille

Contents

Introduction

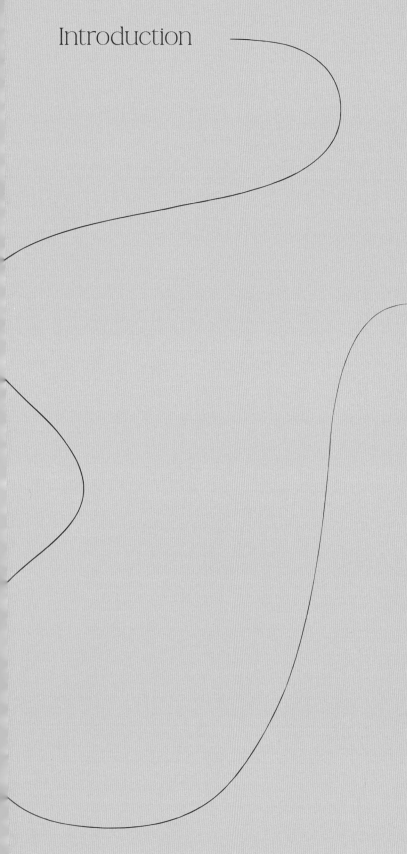

When I first dreamt up the idea of this book, the words that were foremost in my mind as I thrashed out my proposal were simply 'joy' and 'nature'.

I was, at the time, seeking out more cheer after a long and stressful period set against the backdrop of a tumultuous world. It had become my mission to find glimmers of hope where I could, to fight against what felt like a barrage of negativity. And where I found most solace and nearly all of my happiness was in nature, whether swimming in the sparkling sea, walking in bluebell woods or weaving a wreath with stems grown and dried throughout the year. It was this need for joy and the realisation of just how powerful nature can be that led me to put pencil to paper and turn my creative makes and learnings into this book.

In many ways, this book feels like the culmination of a winding journey, deeply intertwined with nature and with flowers in particular. Growing and creating have been two constants throughout my life, evolving over time to become the foundation of my business. These days I spend my time tending to the greenhouse and garden (along with all the admin and chores of running a business), nurturing the flowers and stems that will later become part of a creative idea. Time spent in the studio allows me to translate these homegrown stems into works of art, crafting beauty from the essence of nature itself. I feel so lucky and full of gratitude to have arrived at this point in my journey and to be able to share some of my favourite ideas and projects with you in this book, many of which reflect my earliest explorations with flowers.

During a particularly challenging time in my life – as a new mother to my second baby, Arlo, feeling stifled in my job and surrounded by the chaos of renovating a new house – I found myself in a dark place mentally. Around that time I felt an irresistible pull towards the outdoors, to our new garden. In early March, we brought Arlo home at a time when Mother Nature herself was birthing a new season. Nurturing a new baby while tending to a fledgling garden became my solace. As the garden blossomed with spring flowers, each bloom evoked memories of childhood: lily of the valley, bluebells and toadflax. I felt a stirring within me. I found myself reconnecting with the garden in a way I hadn't experienced since my childhood home and my grandmother's garden.

That year, the garden and nature became my healers, offering refuge and renewal amid the challenges. In fostering new life, both in my family and in my garden, I discovered a deep sense of connection and purpose, reminding me of the power of nature to soothe, heal and inspire. It was around this time that I began to share photos and stories of the flowers that were blooming on my doorstep on Instagram. I found myself captivated by the incredible beauty that others were sharing in these digital squares. Falling headfirst down the rabbit hole of curated images and storytelling, I discovered a shared excitement and passion for capturing the beauty of blooms, in particular dried flowers which were rapidly becoming my obsession.

As I styled and captured images of the changing seasons, each flower became a character in a story, each photograph a chapter in the narrative of my journey. The first image I shared on the platform was a yellow rose that graced our front garden; I can still recall its intoxicating scent, the fragrance mesmerising. Immersing myself in this virtual world, I found a community of like-minded nature lovers, each sharing their own unique perspective and experience. I had stumbled upon my tribe, a group of flower-loving souls who saw the world through the same lens of wonder and appreciation for the natural world.

In the quiet moments while Arlo slept, I would wander through our small garden, carefully selecting stems to transform into flat lays or delicate bud vase displays. Each creation brought me immeasurable pleasure, sparking a newfound sense of artistry and exploration. This period of experimentation and discovery became the foundation of my creative journey. It was a purely visionary time, with no expectations or required outcomes – just the freedom to create for the sake of it.

And so, here I am! Eight years later, I am sharing my projects, learnings, and practices that have helped me find my way. I hope that this book will serve as inspiration for you to step outside and open your eyes to the boundless beauty and wonder that nature offers. May these pages guide you to forge a deeper connection with nature and immerse yourself in creative play which nourishes the soul. The world of plants is a bountiful gift. Take from it what you need, with mindfulness and gratitude, and allow positivity to flow into your life.

Looking back, I cherish those moments, for they were the catalyst towards the changes I so desperately needed to make: to step away from the corporate world and into a life led by nature and creativity.

How to Use This Book

This book is intended as both an inspiration and a practical guide and is carefully crafted to mirror the ebb and flow of the seasons. The 20 projects have been curated and arranged in a way that will encourage you to immerse yourself in the rhythms of nature. Just as we engage with seasonal cooking, this book embraces seasonal creating. Each chapter reflects a moment in time, beckoning you to step outside, gather the gifts of the season, and weave them into a thing of beauty.

For each season I share a range of projects to try out and suggest available flowers, stems and seedheads to use. But please know that you don't have to follow these recommendations to the letter; in fact, I would much prefer you to set your imagination free and choose from what you have and what is available around you. This freedom will allow you to discover what works and what you love, and is part of the process to help you find your style and make each creation uniquely yours.

You will find lots of useful information on key subjects such as how to dry flowers and where to source natural materials. For the most part, the project and ideas in this book require little more than a short stroll outside to gather materials. However, it is important to remain respectful when foraging: ensure that you do not take cuttings from private grounds or dig up plants from public parks; be aware of the sustainability of your surroundings and don't take more than the plant can recover from; try to step lightly in nature, and take care not to damage the host plant. These are some important principles to follow when foraging, but do ensure you research the rules in your locality before embarking on a foraging trip.

All of the projects are demonstrated in a clear, straightforward way, and many are intentionally designed to be simple so that you can pick the book up and be inspired to create, even in the busiest of moments. There is an abundance of creative designs for you to explore and enjoy, each reflecting the changes occurring outdoors. I recommend starting your creative journey at the point in the year that aligns with your current season.

Throughout the book you will find guidance on ways to (re)connect with the natural world, from activities to immerse yourself in the changing seasons to practical tips on what to observe and appreciate and ideas for bringing nature into your home. As you open your eyes to the world around, you will uncover the peaks and troughs of the yearly cycle, from the tranquillity of winter to summer's abundance. And you will learn how to navigate these shifting landscapes and discover the hidden gems nestled within each season.

In essence, this book is a celebration of the art of noticing – a gentle reminder to take small snippets of time each day to reconnect, slow down, notice the subtle changes that occur almost every day, and savour the special moments that nature gifts us. My hope is that each project offers not only a creative outlet but also this moment of connection and mindfulness. Above all, my greatest wish is for this book to bring joy and creativity into your life. Working with nature offers a blank canvas where there are no rights or wrongs, no rigid rules or expectations. I encourage you to release any self-imposed pressures and simply have fun.

I suggest you start small when implementing changes or adopting new practices in your life. It has been shown that setting realistic goals and taking incremental steps leads to greater success in forming new habits. By proceeding gradually, you can avoid feeling overwhelmed and stay focused on your journey of connection and discovery.

Equipment You May Need

Crafting with flowers can be as simple and as affordable as you want it to be. This is perhaps one of the reasons I fell so easily into it, it's so simple to get started and then to keep that momentum going with very little initial outlay. You don't need a huge amount of equipment to begin, and it's likely that you will have many of the items I recommend here already tucked away in your kitchen drawers or garden shed. These are a few things that I simply can't live without and which will make these projects easier to complete.

- ~ Fabric scissors
- ~ Garden snips
- ~ Florist's scissors
- ~ Twine/string
- ~ Wire in various gauges
- ~ Vessels
- ~ Hammer
- ~ Nails
- ~ Pins

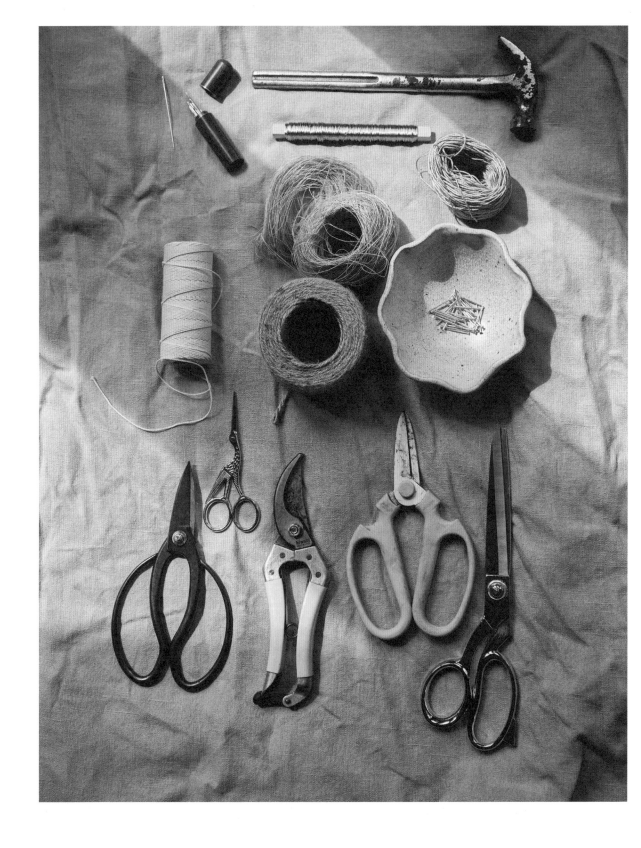

Sourcing Creatively

In my new home in Devon I am lucky enough to have ample space to grow much of what I need for my business and creative projects. That hasn't always been the case though: I lived in Amsterdam for two years, where I did my gardening on a rooftop terrace, then more recently back in the UK within the confines of a small town garden, so I know the frustrations first-hand of sourcing blooms and plants. If you don't have a garden, or perhaps haven't yet begun your growing journey, there are still many ways to find plants and flowers to work with. I'm sharing my best creative tips with you here, to ensure that no matter the space or resources you have available, you can produce something special.

Garden centres and nurseries

When it comes to sourcing plants and bulbs, garden centres and nurseries are excellent starting points. Most towns and cities have conveniently located garden centres, and these days there are numerous online nurseries that offer direct delivery to your doorstep. Look for plants in 9 cm (3½ in) pots or buy packs of six or 12 plant pots as these sizes are perfect for many projects, such as Kokedama (the Japanese art of growing plants in a moss ball, see page 42) and living wreaths. Additionally, garden centres are great places to find bulbs for forcing, and all you need to get them started is a sunny windowsill.

Community groups

Local communities can be a treasure trove of resources for creative projects. I often turn to my local Facebook groups to find items that may be hard to come by through traditional channels. Over the years, I've become more confident in asking for specific materials or plants when needed, and I'm always ready to offer something in return. For instance, the magnolia branch featured in Forcing Blossom Branches (see page 72) was sourced after I reached out on a local WhatsApp group and my friend Amy generously offered me one. We sometimes hesitate to ask for help or make connections, fearing rejection, but I've found that people are generally eager to assist and enjoy being part of creative endeavours.

Flower markets

If you live in a city then you are likely lucky enough to live near a flower market. Flower markets are an amazing source of inspiration, even just to walk around, and a great place to pick up special stems and flowers to work with. I miss my Saturdays in Amsterdam spent strolling through the Noordermarkt, selecting blossom branches and bunches of tulips to take home. One of my favourite markets in the UK is east London's Columbia Road, which is where I gathered many of the flowers that decorated the tables at my wedding.

Flower farming networks

In the UK, we are fortunate to have the wonderful organisation Flowers from the Farm (see page 174). This collective of flower farmers, florists and growers spans the length of Britain and provides an excellent resource for sourcing locally grown flowers. If you're located outside of the UK, I recommend researching similar networks in your area to connect with local growers and sellers of seasonal blooms. Or if there is no such resource in your area, then head to Google to search nearby businesses. Build up your relationship with your contacts, who will in time learn exactly what you love in flowers and may make special accommodations for you.

Florists and supermarkets

Both florists and supermarkets can be excellent places to source flowers. As you become more familiar with the seasons, you'll develop a sense of what's in season and what isn't. However, if you're unsure, it's always worth checking the origins of the flowers you're purchasing. Whenever possible, opt for local blooms to reduce the carbon footprint of your purchase and support nearby growers and farmers. I know that sometimes this isn't possible, so when it isn't, try to apply seasonality to your purchases. Red roses have no place in our homes in deepest winter, just as exotic flowers from far flung tropical zones feel out of place. Stick to the flowers that you can name and recognise as being in season in your locale.

Foraging

Foraging can be a wonderful way to gather inspiration from your surroundings, whether it's a gnarly windfallen branch or a statuesque seedhead. However, there are important rules to follow when foraging, some of which are common sense and others are mandated by law. These rules can vary depending on where you are in the world, so it's essential to research local regulations before heading out to forage. Here are some guidelines that are specific to the UK:

— *Respect:* we share the natural world with many others and it's important to respect the plants that we take from. Give thanks to each and every one of them as you cut from their stems
— *A few, not many:* never strip a plant bare of its flowers or fruits, take one for you and leave the rest for the birds and animals and for it to set seed
— *Invasive species:* should be left alone and never cut from to ensure we don't aid the spread of them; if you are unsure, don't take it
— *Cutting responsibly:* this means not causing harm to the main stem and never cutting too much; if you are cutting more than you are leaving, then that is too much
— *Protected species:* never take from a species that is protected by law. These plants are protected for a reason and the laws are there to ensure they maintain their presence and beauty for generations to come. Ensure you check local laws before picking
— *Where and where not to go:* don't take from private property (even if it's hanging over a wall), or from sites of special interest or National Trust sites, and never cut from public parks – those flowers and plants are for everyone to enjoy
— *Leave the plant intact:* never pull a plant up by its roots

Foraging is an innate part of human nature, and in much the same way as we would forage for blackberries and windfall apples in the autumn, so too should we feel able to gather a few stems of grass or branches when they speak to us. Just do so mindfully and with respect.

Preserving
Nature

1

Drying Flowers

Many of the projects in this book use dried flowers and it's these blooms that started my journey. So, whether you are growing flowers yourself, foraging or sourcing fresh flowers that then need to be dried, these tips and tricks will help you get started on your drying journey.

Harvesting flowers to dry

As a general rule you should be harvesting or cutting your flowers to dry when they are at their peak. This differs from when cutting fresh flowers, which are mostly harvested at the cracked bud stage (where they have swelling flower buds, with one or two just beginning to open). The reason for this is because we want the flowers to dry with their faces fully open; if they are cut too early they can be tricky to dry as the buds are too fleshy. Choose a dry day to harvest your flowers, and ideally one that isn't too hot. Cut your stems and leave them somewhere cool and dry to have a good drink in a bucket of water overnight; this helps the flowers to recover from the stress of being cut before they are hung out to dry. During the harvesting process, remove the majority of the leaves from the stems as these can be unsightly when dried and can also go mouldy.

If you are not growing your own flowers and want to have a go at drying a bunch gifted from a loved one or bought from the supermarket, then you'll need to assess the stage of the flowers before you hang them out to dry. We are looking for a flower that is fully opened and in bloom to dry, so if your flowers arrive with you at the closed bud stage, place them in a vase with water in a warmish place (not too hot, the house is fine) to open up. Once the flowers have opened, they can then be hung out to dry in the same way as if you have harvested them. The important thing is that the flowers are not allowed to 'go over', which happens if they are left in the vase (or on the stem) for days once they have opened. Leaving them too long can result in the petals dropping and even turning brown as they begin to fade away.

Which flowers dry well?

Nearly all flowers can be dried, with a few exceptions. However, not all flowers are as beautiful dried as they are when fresh; though this is also subjective, and what I find captivating and beautiful in a dried flower could greatly vary from what others might appreciate. Part of the wonderful process of drying is experimentation and the discovery of what it is you enjoy, both to look at and work with. As the seasons advance from spring through to autumn there are more and more plants to be found that dry well. Early spring offers us fleshy, bouncy blooms such as tulips and narcissi, and while these are incredibly beautiful dried, they sadly do not last, often falling from the stem once they have dried. I will often gather these petals up and display them in a shallow handcrafted ceramic bowl as potpourri.

Once summer arrives and the hardy annuals and perennials return to us alongside grasses and, later on, statuesque seedheads, this is when the harvesting can really begin in earnest. When assessing a flower for its drying potential, consider the fleshiness of its petals and also its stems. The woodier the stem and the more papery the petal, the more likely it is to dry well: consider the strawflower as a best-case example of a flower that will dry well.

MY FAVOURITE (AND EASIEST) PLANTS TO DRY

Achillea (yarrow)
Gypsophila (baby's breath) (best dried standing upright in a vase with just a little water at the base)
Xerochrysum (strawflowers)
Hydrangeas (best dried standing upright in a vase with just a little water at the base)
Delphinium (larkspur)
Nigella seedheads Limonium (statice)
Alchemilla mollis (lady's mantle)
Phalaris canariensis (canary grass)
Briza maxima (greater quaking grass)
Chrysanthemums
Ranunculus
Buttercups
Leucanthemum vulgare (oxeye daisies)

Where to dry

I have a whole studio dedicated to drying flowers, but this has not always been the case. In our old house I dried my flowers inside, hanging from a branch on a wall in our living space. If you are short on space, you could do the same, creating a hanging branch on which to dry your flowers. Here's a simple guide to creating your own dried-flower hanging branch:

1 *Select a branch:* choose a sturdy branch with interesting shapes and textures. Look for one with multiple offshoots or interesting knots and bends that will provide plenty of space for hanging flowers.
2 *Prepare the branch:* trim any excess twigs or foliage, leaving behind a clean and visually appealing structure.
3 *Attach hanging material:* cut twine, rope or ribbon to the desired length, ensuring it is long enough to loop over a nail or hook on your wall. Tie one end of each piece securely to each end of the branch, leaving enough slack to create a gentle curve when hung.
4 *Hang on the wall:* choose a suitable location to hang the branch, and use nails, hooks or adhesive wall hangers to secure it in place, ensuring it is level and stable.
5 *Dry your flowers:* you can begin drying flowers by simply hanging them from the offshoots or loops of twine. Arrange the flowers in small bunches or individually, spacing them out to allow for air circulation and to prevent them going mouldy.

How to dry

I dry the majority of my flowers by hanging them upside down: it is the simplest and most effective method. I tend to tie bunches of five to ten stems (depending upon the size and scale of the flowers) together using a simple looped knot which can be tightened easily. The string is then tied together at the end and looped over my branch or chicken wire using a very simple S-shaped hook, created using sturdy garden wire. This makes for easy moving once the flowers have dried.

To hang flowers out to dry successfully, there are just a few simple conditions to consider. The tips I am sharing here also apply to how you store your flowers once they are dried.

1 *Sunlight:* while you don't necessarily need to dry your flowers in the dark (I don't, my studio has windows on all sides), it is important that they don't dry in direct sunlight. Direct sunlight can cause the flowers to fade and turn brittle, which will make them tricky to work with.
2 *Moisture:* flowers dry best in a space that is free from moisture and damp. If you remember that we are trying to extract the moisture from the flowers, it makes sense that we will need a nice dry space in which to do this. Therefore it's best to avoid kitchens, where the steam from the stove could be problematic, as well as bathrooms. Outside spaces such as sheds can be fine if we have a nice hot summer, but the flowers will need to be monitored regularly in case damp starts to set in.
3 *Temperature:* when drying flowers we are looking for an ambient temperature, not too hot and not too cold. We want the flowers to dry out at a steady pace, over time. If the space is too hot and they dry too quickly they can become brittle; and equally, if it's too cold they can take too long to dry out and that results in mould and damp setting in.

Sand Drying

This method is particularly good for drying delicate blooms that would otherwise be tricky to dry while retaining their beauty. The sand acts like a sponge, pulling the moisture out from the flowers while also holding their petals, leaves and stems in position, resulting in the most perfect dried blooms: it's like magic. I have used silica gel in the past for this but was unhappy with the impact on the environment, so have recently shifted to using sand. The best sand to use is a very fine sand, often sold as 'chinchilla powder' (it's used as a dust bath to remove mites from their fur). I remain in awe of flowers dried in this way, as they appear nearly identical to when they were fresh when lifted out of the sand.

Fill a Tupperware container (the same size or bigger than the flowers you wish to dry) with a layer of sand, carefully lay your chosen flower down and gradually cover with another layer of sand until the flower is completely covered. Leave for a few weeks in a dry, warm space before carefully lifting out the flowers to reveal their preserved beauty.

The only downside of using this method to dry flowers is that they can often reabsorb moisture from the air. This can result in them flopping and turning brown, so it is best to store them somewhere warm and dry for longevity.

FLOWERS THAT DRY WELL
USING THIS METHOD

Violas
Cosmos
Toadflax
Rudbeckia
Roses
Buttercups

Pressing Flowers

Preserving flowers by pressing them is a centuries-old activity, and one that was used in the past to help botanists document their studies of plants from near and far. While the technique is still used for scientific purposes, it has also (as far back as the Victorian era) been used as a way to preserve plants for pleasure and fun. Recently, pressed flowers – and art created from them – have experienced a resurgence that is wonderful to witness. It is a particularly good method of drying more delicate flowers such as pansies, violas and snowdrops, and is accessible to us all as little is needed to get started.

How to press flowers

All manner of flower presses can be bought in shops and online, from huge A1-size plywood presses to smaller flower presses created from vintage wooden tie presses. To get started though, you really don't need more than some heavy books or magazines and white cartridge or blotting paper. The main consideration is that there is enough weight in the outer layers (whether that's plywood with bolts and nuts or piles of magazines) to press flower specimens flat to the papers they are sandwiched between.

Pick your flowers on a dry day, but if this isn't possible then spend some time – before pressing them and after cutting – drying off any excess moisture with absorbent kitchen towel or a tea towel. Choose the very best of your flowers to press, as each and every imperfection will show up with this method of drying, and the devil really is in the detail. While the odd nibble out of a petal here and there can be cute and add charm, it's best to select the most complete flowers to press.

MY FAVOURITE
FLOWERS TO PRESS

Forget-me-not
Pansy
Viola (these can be pressed with
   the roots intact)
Snake's head fritillary
Buttercup
Sweet pea
Bluebell*
Snowdrop*
Poppy

*These should not be picked from
the wild, only from what you grow.

1. Begin by removing any leaves that are going to hinder the pressing process; these may be ones that are sitting across the stem or will get squashed under others. Leave a few leaves on, particularly for pansies and forget-me-nots, where they add to the appearance of the plant.

2. Next lay the flower face down on the chosen paper, gently pressing it in position and helping any petals and leaves spread out on the page.

3. Continue to fill the page with flowers, ensuring that none of the petals or leaves overlap, as this can cause them to stick together and tarnish the finished pressed flowers.

4. Once all the flowers are in place, take another sheet of paper and lay it over the top of the flowers, carefully pressing it in place.

5. Now close your press or book/magazine, tightening the screws or piling more books and magazines on top.

Most flowers will dry within a few weeks, and you can check on their progress by carefully lifting the sheets of paper to take a peek. Once they are all dried, lift the top sheet of paper off and, using tweezers, carefully lift each flower off the bottom sheet of paper. They can stick a little in the middle of the flower so take great care lifting there to avoid petals being torn or yanked off. Pressed flowers can be stored in large envelopes in a drawer to use when creative inspiration strikes.

Nature Tables

I have fond memories from childhood of nature tables in classrooms, cluttered with treasures collected by myself and classmates. The thrill of discovering a shiny conker nestled within its spiky shell, and the joy of sharing that experience with others, remains vivid in my mind. Although nature tables have largely disappeared from schools, sadly overshadowed by a shift towards academic subjects, children continue to find awe and wonder in the natural world. My own boys still delight in filling their pockets with feathers and sticks during our walks.

Recently, I've found myself revisiting the concept of nature tables, creating my own makeshift versions at home. This newfound appreciation began during lockdown, when our family embarked on more outdoor adventures than ever before. As we travelled through fields and woodlands, my boys eagerly gathered lichen-covered sticks and intricately shaped stones, each deserving of its own space to be admired. I love to create spaces for these treasures in my home and studio.

Ways to display nature tables

You don't need a lot of room to create a nature table, and they can become a focal point of interest for the family and visitors. At one of my pottery sessions I created an open shelving unit with shelves and holes of various sizes for nestling treasures in. I keep this hanging above the desk where I work, as a source of inspiration. There are numerous other options for displaying a nature altar. Consider repurposing an old printer's block or a vintage glass cabinet, or simply setting aside a space on a windowsill. The key is to choose a location that invites exploration and reflection, allowing the beauty of nature to infuse your living space with its magic.

IDEAS FOR THINGS TO INCLUDE IN YOUR NATURE TABLE

There are so many wonderful nature items that can be featured in altars. Here are some of my favourite finds:

Skeleton leaves
Old, abandoned birds' nest (only take these if you know for sure that the bird has left the nest)
Lichen
Shells from the beach
Hag stones (stones with holes all the way through them)
Special feathers
Dried seedheads

Nature Flat Lays

When I first began capturing images of my flowers, flat lays were one of my favourite ways to do so. In essence, flat lays are top-down photographs capturing a scene composed of carefully arranged objects on a flat surface, each telling its own story through its intentional placement. Flat lays have been used as a way to display botanical material for centuries, but their popularity has surged thanks their use on social media. They have been embraced by artists and design professionals alike as a means to showcase their work and as sources of inspiration.

When used to capture plants, they can be reminiscent of herbariums (collections of dried plant specimens that are stored, catalogued and arranged by family, genus and species for study) and of botanical identifier books.

I've dedicated countless hours to crafting flat lays, using them not only to sharpen my photography skills but also to refine my ability to harmonise stems and flowers in a way that resonates. Over time, flat lays have become an integral part of my routine, serving to document the ever-changing beauty of my garden and the shifting seasons. In the act of creating these visual narratives, I find myself grounded in the present moment, often slipping into a state of flow as I delicately arrange flowers together, mindful of their fleeting nature.

How to capture a flat lay

— *Lighting:* as with all photography, lighting is important and natural lighting is the best. I'm fortunate to have incredible natural lighting in my studio and I tend to position my boards or material just below the source of light (in this case east-facing windows) with the top of the image closest to the window, which is preferable to being side-lit. A slightly overcast day is best, as bright sunshine can cause shadows and oversaturation.
— *Backdrops:* the key is for there to be interest in the textures of the backdrop but for them to not overpower the objects that you are placing on them. Naturally dyed material works really well, although it will need to be ironed before use as any creases or imperfections tend to show up. Canvas sheets painted using limewash are another great option, as are old sheets of scrap metal, which often have incredible patinated edges.

As with all things nature-related, there aren't really any hard and fast rules to abide by when working on a flat lay, but it's worth paying attention to a few things to help with cohesiveness:

— *Colour palette:* I find it best to work with colours that complement each other, steering clear of anything that will jar or stand out. For example, avoid including a red tulip if your chosen palette is soft and neutral
— *Sometimes a flower or stem won't sit in exactly the position we need it to;* it's OK to remove a flower from the stem to encourage it to lay flat for the photograph
— *When laying your stems out on the surface, look for visual connections between them;* often I will look for a triangle shape of three of the same flowers, or the texture of a leaf complementing the focal flower
— *Negative space:* this plays a crucial role in enhancing the interconnectedness of each element, creating visual harmony and depth within the frame

Following the Seasons

I adore the changing seasons, each bringing its own delights and challenges. A few years ago I hosted a two-day workshop in my Devon studio for a student from Manila in the Philippines. On the first day she commented on how much the English talk about the weather. I laughed and explained that as an island nation Britain is heavily influenced by the weather and experiences seasons that change quickly. It was a hot, balmy day in late September and my bones were yearning for autumn to arrive, but summer was clinging on for dear life. Coming from a place where there are largely two seasons (wet and dry – both warm) my student was fascinated by the myriad changes, and I felt lucky to live in a country where the seasons are felt so acutely.

It's incredible how the changing seasons have the power to evoke such deep and meaningful memories. The sight of the first cherry blossoms or the scent of sweet peas can transport us back in time, stirring emotions and recollections that feel as vivid as if they happened just yesterday. These connections with nature are intertwined with our personal experiences, becoming a part of who we are and shaping our perceptions. It's a beautiful reminder of the richness and depth of our relationship with the natural world and the ways in which it continues to influence and inspire us throughout our lives.

This book, and so much of my work, has been inspired by the seasons. So much of my time is spent in the garden – watching, growing, willing plants to flower and appreciating their beauty when they arrive – that it is impossible to not be influenced by nature's cycles. In the same way that fruit and vegetables out of season have less flavour and less character, I feel similarly about flowers and plants. I find it jarring to see bouquets of summer flowers like sunflowers and gerberas in the supermarket as I do my weekly shop in the middle of spring. We have become so accustomed to having exactly what we want whenever we want it that for many it's hard to know what is seasonal. Following the seasons and appreciating what each one has to offer helps us stay connected to the natural world and also encourages us to enjoy its fleeting delights. It's this ephemeral nature that makes everything so much more special and unique, meaning we can look forward to a flower or vegetable arriving and enjoy it all the more knowing that in a few weeks we will be saying goodbye to it for another year.

Since moving deeper into the countryside I have been keeping a daily diary of happenings in the garden, documenting each change that a new week or even day brings. Noticing these daily shifts has shown me the dramatic differences between, for example, early spring and late spring. It has helped me remain rooted in the moment and has become my favourite way to start the morning; herbal tea in hand I will stroll around the garden to see what new face greets me, moving back inside to dutifully note all the new finds and discoveries in my journal.

Though we think of the four seasons as winter, spring, summer and autumn, I often feel this is such a simplistic way of viewing the cycle of the year. I have begun to notice that so much can happen within one season, such dramatic changes to our landscape and experiences.

I've become fascinated by the Japanese approach to seasons, where they follow 72 seasons in a year. In the Japanese calendar they honour the same four seasons as the UK does, and then expand upon these by splitting each season into six parts to create 24 'sekki' – each one roughly 15 days long. These periods reflect the Chinese lunar and solar calendar. These sekki are further divided into three micro-seasons or 'ko', each lasting for five days.

Every one of these micro-seasons reflects the minute changes of Japan's ecosystem. Of course these micro-seasons fluctuate greatly with the weather, and even more so as climate change becomes an even bigger influence. Each of the micro-seasons is given a name relating to the activity or experience that is reflected or happening at that time, which makes it less about dates (like seasons in the UK) and more about the changes that are actually taking place in nature.

It's the noticing and anticipation that I love the most about the idea of 72 seasons: pausing to reflect, to look and listen, and to experience those changes that are happening all around us in the natural world can be the most beautiful way to stay connected and grounded. It helps to show us how resilient nature is, and we are: no matter the weather, no matter the storms that pass through, the flowers will still grow and the plants will still flourish. I have also found, in darker times, that this daily act of noticing has helped me to understand that everything is transient.

MY FAVOURITES FROM JAPAN'S 72 SEASONS (WHICH QUITE OFTEN APPLY IN THE UK TOO)

Rain moistens the soil (19–23 Feb)
Mist starts to linger (24–28 Feb)
Sparrows start to nest
   (21–25 March)
First cherry blossoms
   (26–30 March)
What ripens and is harvested
   (31 May–5 June)
Earth is damp, air is humid
   (29 July–22 August)
Dew glistens white on grass
   (8–12 September)
Cold sets in, winter begins
   (7–11 December)

2

Emergence

Spring has to be the most eagerly anticipated and longed for of all the seasons; I know it is for me.

When spring emerges from the depths of winter I am reminded of how wonderful it is to live in the countryside. Winter can feel punishing and relentless, and after months of the cold, wet weather and endless mud, the first shoots of spring are so very welcome.

Spring arrives with new growth in the garden and the hedgerows, together with a shift in the light and a raising of the tempo in the garden. The dawn chorus is deafening as birds call for mates, protecting their territory for the breeding season to come. Crows return to build their nest again in our tall Scots pine, terrorising the mistle thrush and sneaking newts from the pond to feast on. Owls call to each other across the garden and down into the valley, their haunting cries echoing around the land. There is life and movement and excitement all around.

Spring likes to tease, jostling with the remnants of winter for dominance. When March arrives, I have this big expectation that so do warmer days, green shoots and all the flowers, but things take time. Snow can still fall in March and frosts regularly occur on a clear night. Winter is not over just yet, and each day feels like a tug of war not yet won by either season. Spring is nurturing, volatile, exciting and frustrating all at once, doing exactly as she wants when she wants. Sometimes we are offered up four seasons in one day, and when all feels lost, we are gifted a first sunny day where warmth can be felt on our depleted skin, and all is forgiven.

First shoots

Spring is when the Earth's cycle begins once again, and with it comes an uncontrollable energy. Plants that have lain dormant for so many months stir with life, and I feel this energy in my body, too. The hope that accompanies spring is palpable; all memories of winter and any failures of the past year slip away as the anticipation of a new year begins.

It's a busy month in the garden, with so many seeds to be sown and a constant shifting of seedlings in the greenhouse, monitoring light levels and temperatures to ensure they get exactly what they need. The excitement that accompanies the first signs of green shoots popping up from seed trays is like no other. Spring can, however, feel exhausting at times: whereas in winter I had time to ponder and reflect, spring propels me into busy days with not enough hours to get things done. The garden can't wait, and along with sowing seeds there are many jobs that, if they don't get done on time, may as well be left until the next year. Mulching continues, and staking plants and getting a handle on any weeds that appear is critical. The to-do list is never-ending, but my heart and head are so happy to be busy. As the days get longer, I find myself spending more and more time outside; incrementally, the old rhythm of gardening until dark and starting my day with sunrise has returned.

In our garden, on the first full moon of spring – sometimes as early as February but often in March –frogs and toads march to the pond to mate. I throw open the back door to let the dogs out to a deafening chorus of croaks. Within days, the pond swells with clumps of frogspawn, the lily pads wound tightly together with strings of toad spawn. My boys wait patiently for the tadpoles to hatch, and later in the year watch as they make their journey on four legs out of the pond.

Blossom and bloom

In early spring the blossoms return, with magnificent magnolias bursting into flower and delicate cherry blossoms following closely behind. Flowers emerge on the bare branches of trees with force and vitality, showing us what resilience is. I pray for calm weather so we can savour the blossoms for as long as possible, without them being whipped away by the angry spring winds that sometimes visit.

After the blossoms come the narcissi and the tulips, a juxtaposition of blousy blooms sitting alongside the delicate wildflowers that appear in meadows and along banks seemingly overnight. Old favourites of mine include snake's head fritillaries, with their chequered coats and bobbing heads, forget-me-nots for their vibrant flash of blue, and cowslips, elegant in their delicate yellow beauty.

Each winter I plant more and more bulbs in the garden. I have an insatiable appetite for spring bulbs and the joy they bring. In the depths of winter it feels like time well spent digging the hard ground to nestle in an unassuming brown bulb packed so full of life. This winter I filled zinc planters and pots with hundreds of narcissi and tulips and positioned them outside our kitchen door. They offer the most perfect view from our kitchen table, and each time I go out to feed the birds I can enjoy their enchanting fragrance. I have learnt over the years how valuable it is to plan planting so that it can be viewed when in the house. As this past winter and spring have been particularly grey and miserable, it's been uplifting to see such vividness as we eat breakfast.

Grow

I can be impatient to get growing when March arrives, and days spent poring over seed catalogues and thinking of starting the cycle all over again is intoxicating. I have to be patient, waiting until light levels are high enough and a little warmth returns to the soil. Sometime in mid-March I begin to sow seeds again and the greenhouse becomes my solace on dark days. No matter how many times I do this, I get the same rush of excitement with the new shoots.

In late April I begin to notice that the trees are cloaked in vivid greens and reds; it's like a second autumn. Walking among the bluebell woods I am captivated by the spectacle of these beautiful flowers en masse, made even more dramatic set against the backdrop of viridescent beech trees, new leaves bursting forth. By May the flowers are coming thick and fast. I don't want to miss a thing and my walks around the garden become less focused on the detail and more about the sheer wonder of how on earth these plants have managed to grow centimetres in what feels like days. The wildflower lawn is gaining height and the first of the oxeye daisies are budding up. The perennial beds are full, these plants filling out nicely in anticipation of warm summer days just around the corner.

Whereas in winter my daily journal documents very slow changes, the pages now fill with records of each flower that opens, each seedling that germinates and the endless changes to the weather. My daily walks are filled with wonder as the old Devon banks that flank our road become an incredible tapestry of wildflowers, billowing cow parsley overshadowing the bluebells and red campion.

As my greenhouse fills up with seedlings, my studio begins to empty of the flowers from last year. I am focused on growing, and it's with some relief that orders for dried flowers begin to slow down. There are times in the year when my love of everlastings abates: with so much new life outside they feel less attractive somehow, but my heart will be back with them soon. The house begins to fill with fresh flowers, and the flower press fills up with all their delicate beauty. I lean into every last moment of this season, and bringing flowers inside feels like the biggest gift after winter. Summer is knocking at May's door now, where green will give way to a riot of colour.

Kokedama

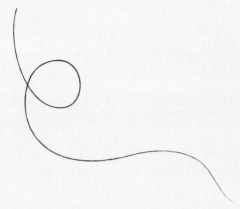

I must confess to being a bit of a houseplant addict. Our living room often resembles a jungle and I'm forever propagating baby plants to add to our collection. I hang plants from the ceiling, wind their tendrils along walls and shelves and dot clusters of pots on windowsills and in corners. Each winter I bring my geraniums indoors to spend the colder days on a ledge above my desk, and often they will flower in the depths of winter, filling my heart with anticipation for what's to come.

Translated as moss (koke) ball (dama), these are a beautiful, stylish way to bring plants inside. Their roots are firmly in the culture of Japan, where these plant sculptures have been created since the early 1600s. Kokedama embody the wonderful principles of wabi sabi, which is an awareness of the transient nature of earthly things. The author Andrew Juniper defines wabi sabi as 'an intuitive appreciation of ephemeral beauty in the physical world that reflects the irreversible flow of life in the spiritual world.'

The chosen plants are carefully wrapped in a blanket of compost and then moss to keep them moist and fed, with the outer layer of moss visually becoming part of the plant itself, a living structure. I have many kokedama dotted around my house, and they thrive especially well in the bathroom, where regular steaming from the shower serves them well. Ferns adapt particularly well with this method, as do spider plants (baby ones before they grow monstrous!) and orchids.

In spring, when the bulbs are out and all the baby plants are getting going, I enjoy crafting kokedama out of the first of the flowers and bringing them inside to enjoy. I hang them above my desk so it feels as if I am working in a garden when sat at my laptop. If you decide to create some of these beauties using spring flowers, once they have finished flowering they can be planted complete in the garden to flower again the following spring. If you prefer, you can dismantle the moss ball and only pop the bulbs or plant in the garden. Both methods will work fine.

Once your kokedama have been created you can either hang them or sit them on a saucer in their final position. To water, give them a regular spritz (daily is best) and at least once a week submerge them in a bowl of water – but be sure to allow them to drain fully before hanging them back out again. It's amazing how much moisture the moss can absorb and hold onto. For my houseplant kokedama that are going to be in situ for months and quite possibly years, I give them a seaweed feed during their growing season in much the same way as you would a normal houseplant. I tend to not bother doing this with my spring kokedama, as they often only last a month or so before being planted outside.

Gather

- ~ Plants: I have used violas and muscari
- ~ Compost mix: here I have used SylvaGrow mixed with vermiculite and some garden soil to help it clump
- ~ String or twine
- ~ Moss: I gathered mine from the garden but you can lift it from the woods

Method

1   Mix your compost base in a container and give it a squeeze to check whether it holds together. It's helpful to have a compost mix that forms a solid mass to encourage it to gather and clump around the root ball of the plant.

2   Lay your moss out on the surface in front of you to form a mat of moss, the idea being that you can then wrap this around the ball of the plant.

3   Remove the plant from its pot and carefully bulk out the root ball with your compost mix, encouraging the mix to encase the roots. It can be tricky and often I have had to use the moss to hold the soil in place. You want to give the plant just enough energy from the compost mix to keep it going a month or so while it is hanging.

4   Wind a long piece of string around the moss base, covering as much of the surface area as possible to keep the plant neatly in position. Secure with a knot.

5   Wrap another length of string around the moss ball base and secure both ends towards the top of the moss ball where the plant sits. You are aiming for the string to be in such a position that the plant sits upright when hanging. This can be tricky, and a few of mine are hanging at a jaunty angle! Think of it as trying to create a handle from which to hang the kokedama.

An Indoor
Flower Garden

When skies are leaden and the ground is thick with mud, indoor gardens are the perfect way to brighten darker days. These small pots of joy are so simple to create and require just a small amount of forethought at the end of the year to fill our homes with fresh flowers in the early part of the next year. They are a pop of colour set against a gloomy backdrop, and in some cases – such as with hyacinths – provide the most incredible aroma, enough to lift anyone out of a slump. I couldn't be without them, and I nestle these pots purposefully around the house to be noticed as I go about my day. Favourite spots include by the bed, particularly for those that have a scent, on the kitchen table and at my desk.

This method of growing flower bulbs is called forcing, where we are creating a safe and welcoming environment for the bulbs to allow them to quickly sprout and bloom (often in as little as 6–8 weeks). Bulbs are quite miraculous in that everything they need to flourish is already stored within the bulb, and this means we can be clever about how we force them. While many of us will be aware of forcing paperwhites (a snowy narcissus) and amaryllis by simply resting the bottom part of the bulb in a shallow bowl of water, any spring bulb can be helped along using this method.

I tend to favour small and delicate blooms over the blousy, shouty ones. Smaller blooms such as crocus can get lost outside unless planted en masse, and so to have them flowering indoors offers the opportunity to really stop and appreciate their intricate beauty. And snake's head fritillaries win my heart every year, their heads gently nodding on divine twisting stems.

Nearly all the bulbs and plants listed on page 50 can be transplanted to the garden once they have flowered and begun to fade. While they may not all be as vigorous or vibrant the next year, they will settle into their new environment and before long will naturalise.

FAVOURITE BULBS
TO FORCE

Grape hyacinths
Narcissi ('golden bells' and 'spoirot'
Snake's head fritillary (mice love the
bulbs of snake's head, so if forcing in
the greenhouse keep them covered)
Crocus (mice also love crocus bulbs!)
Iris reticulata
Paperwhites (these can't be planted
outside as they're not hardy)
Amaryllis (these can sometimes
flower up to three times in one
season, so wait patiently as the first
blooms go over)
Hyacinths
Snowdrops
Snowflakes
Bluebells

Note: Snowdrops, snowflakes and
bluebells can also be forced but do
much better when planted in the
green (when shoots of green have
appeared rather than dormant bulbs
– this goes for when planting out in
the garden too). If I want to bring
snowdrops inside then I will dig up a
clump from the garden just as
the green shoots appear, then replant
as the flowers fade.

Please never dig up snowdrops or
bluebells, or indeed any plants from
the wild – only take from your own
spaces or where you have permission.

Emergence

Gather

- ~ Mushroom trays (optional)
- ~ A selection of pretty pots: I make
  my own and also source from thrift stores
  and vintage stores. I adore the old terracotta
  pots I've used here
- ~ Gravel
- ~ Compost mixed with loam
- ~ Moss

Method

1. I like to start my bulbs off in mushroom trays in the greenhouse before moving them over to pots just before they begin to flower: this helps when growing many bulbs at one time. You can also plant directly into your preferred vessel.

2. Give some consideration to the bulb and vessel combination. For shorter bulbs you will want to select a smaller vessel such as a terracotta pot, and for something like a paperwhite (which can grow very tall) you'll want to use a vessel with more depth and weight.

3. Begin by placing a small layer of gravel at the bottom of your vessel.

4. Fill the rest of the pot with your compost mix, leaving enough space at the top to nestle in your bulbs.

5. Position your bulbs with their roots touching the earth. The bulbs can be placed quite close together, and you can choose to create a mix of flowers or fill each vessel with the same type. Use your imagination and tap into your creative vision.

6. Nestle a small amount of soil in and around the bulbs, but don't entirely cover them.

7. Cover with a layer of gravel or moss, depending on your preference, as this helps the bulbs stay moist and not dry out.

8. Keep the bulbs inside away from the elements to encourage them to grow. The warmer the temperatures, the faster the bulbs will grow and flower. If you have lots of pots, you can stagger where you keep your bulbs so that you have a continuous supply of beautiful blooms through winter and into spring.

9. Some flowers will need supporting as they can grow very tall and top heavy. Paperwhites are the main ones that will need some assistance. You can create support structures using hazel (whose catkins are particularly lovely) and birch twigs, which both complement the flowers.

Ephemerality

Much of my work is centred around preserving flowers, be it drying or pressing, as I try to capture their beauty and essence for as long as I possibly can. While I am captivated by the process of drying flowers and the longevity it provides, I also recognise the inherent beauty in the ephemeral nature of plants. It's a reminder to cherish each bloom and embrace the ever-changing landscape of the natural world.

Flowering poppies on a summer's day epitomise the concept of ephemerality. On warm days, with bright sunlight gracing the skies, a poppy flower unfurls from its tightly held bud, revealing delicate papery petals that dance in the breeze. It welcomes in bees and hoverflies to collect the pollen nestled deep inside the flowers, little legs and bodies rubbing up against the golden yellow dust before flying away heavy with their load. This fleeting beauty is short-lived: within a day, the poppy's petals begin to wilt and drop, as it sets seed to ensure its future. It's a brief but mesmerising display of nature's transient wonders.

From a creative perspective, working with materials that you know with some degree of certainty are not going to last for long can provide a much-needed dose of freedom. As a child, I'd spend hours crafting daisy chains, unconcerned about their inevitable wilting by day's end. It was the act itself, working with my hands, nestled safely among the long grasses, that brought joy. Knowing that time may take away all that we're working on allows us to focus solely on the process at that given moment, and less on the end result. When we free ourselves from expectations of a 'finished' piece, a certain level of playful freedom can be tapped into.

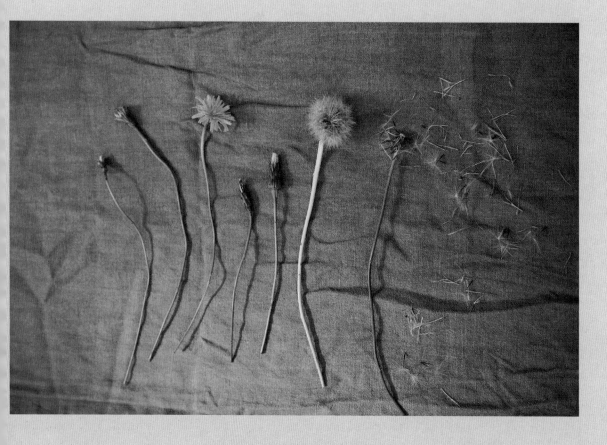

Embrace a fading flower

In spring, I love to fill vases with tulips to watch how their shapes shift and evolve over the weeks, until eventually their petals begin to fade away and drop to the table beneath. I gather up those petals and will spend time studying their gentle curves and the painterly strokes across them. I'm not afraid of things wilting and fading, I like to embrace these changes and enjoy them. The same can be done with narcissi and peonies, which make the most dramatic exit from this world by dropping all of their petals in one final flamboyant act.

Make a daisy chain

Making daisy chains instantly transports me back to childhood, evoking feelings of peace and free spiritedness. In the summertime, when the grass is abundant with the sweet flower heads of lawn daisies, step outside and sit on the grass to enjoy the simple process of piecing together a daisy chain.

To make a daisy chain, pick daisies far down the stem close to the earth so you have a long stem to work with. Pierce a hole in the length of the stem using your thumbnail and then carefully thread the stalk of another daisy through the hole until the head reaches the opening. Continue for as long as you like.

Dandelion clock play

Dandelions are one of the first flowers to arrive in our lawns in early spring, heralding the warmer days with their joyful sunshine faces. They are not always loved, as they tend to be a bit of a thug in the garden, but they are a source of much-needed nectar for early flying insects. Their gossamer 'clock' seedheads are a common sight across meadows in the UK and are an absolute delight to play with. If you pick the seedheads when they are fully out they will simply disperse at the slightest hint of a breeze, however there are ways to work with them to avoid this.

Head out in the morning when the seedheads are yet to open and select those that are tightly closed but with a hint of fluff appearing from the top of the closed seedhead. These can look quite similar to the flower buds themselves, so take some time to get to know the difference. Gather as many stems as you would like to use. Working with the closed seedhead buds, set about creating your vision, whether it's garlands, 'forever dandelion clocks' preserved in jam jars or an installation (thin gauge wire can be used to thread through the base of the closed seedhead to allow them to be hung). As time passes, often within a day, the seedheads will unfurl into fluffy displays of unexpected beauty. However, be mindful that they will eventually disperse entirely, so choose your display locations wisely. No matter your views on dandelions, I promise you will view them in a completely different way after you've seen this magic take place.

Buttercup
Chandelier

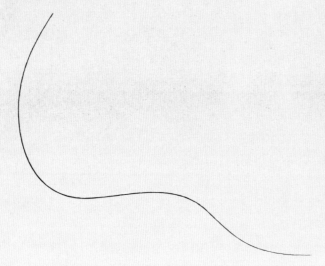

My love for buttercups knows no bounds. When the fields next to our house become a glorious golden sea in late spring, I spend hours watching their delicate heads sway in the breeze, standing tall and proud above the grasses with just the sorrel competing for attention. Even in the dullest springs an abundance of buttercups can lift our spirits, shining with joy no matter what the weather brings.

It's only really in recent years that I have fully taken notice of their beauty; each year I find myself asking if they are especially magnificent this year, or have I just never paid them enough attention before now? Perhaps moving deeper into the countryside has made me notice them more, or maybe their presence has been more appreciated in these past few years, when springs in the UK have been cold and wet, lacking in sunshine.

There are many types of buttercups, but the best for this project and for drying and pressing are field buttercups. These grow on tall stems, which makes them perfect for crafting of all sorts. Field buttercups don't grow from runners, making them a good option for the garden as they tend to be less aggressive. Creeping buttercup, which lies low to the ground and produces flowers on shorter stems, is one to beware of if you are a grower: it is an absolute thug, and I would advise against adding it to your soil.

This buttercup chandelier uses fresh buttercups that go on to dry. Fresh stems are needed as they have flex in them and allow for the stems to be folded over without snapping. While I have used buttercups here, grasses look equally as good, as do oxeye daisies – just remember to always use fresh plants.

The best time to cut buttercups for this project is when most of the flowers on the stem are in flower, with the rest in bud. This tends to be around mid-to-end May, depending on the weather and where you are in the country. As buttercups begin to set seed (so if left that little bit too long before cutting), their petals disperse and flutter to the ground as you cut them, and what we're looking for here is full stems of flowers to give a golden hue all the way around.

Cut the stems and leave them to have a good long drink in a cool place overnight before working with them, as this helps them to be in tip-top condition before you start.

Gather

~ A wreath hoop: here I have used a small
  bamboo hoop, which I like for its extra
  thickness and its texture, which helps when
  adding in the stems, giving a little bit of grip
  to work with
~ Buttercups or other flowers: for this chandelier
  I threaded oxeye daisies in among the
  buttercups to reflect the meadow in my garden
~ Naturally dyed ribbons (see page 128) to hang
  the chandelier

Method

1 Prepare your stems of buttercups, or whichever plant material you have chosen to work with. Remove any leaves (there won't be too many on the buttercups) and cut them to similar lengths: this is down to personal taste, but I like to have a range of lengths within a few centimetres of each other. How long they are is your choice, but will also depend upon the size of your hoop: the bigger the hoop, the longer you may want the plant stems to be.

2 When piecing this together ensure that the flowers are always facing towards the ground, with the stems wrapped around the hoop. Begin by taking a couple of stems in your hand and placing the stems on the outside of the hoop, leaving enough length at the top to create the knot.

3 Carefully fold the top of the stem that is facing towards the sky over the hoop, looping it through the middle and then down towards the ground. Now bend the end you are working with forward towards you before carefully looping it back over the top part of the stems.

4 Keep hold of everything very tightly with one hand while you add in more stems with the other.

5 Add in your next bunch of stems, positioning them on the hoop in the same was as you did before, but this time ensure they are sitting over the folded ends of the original knot. This serves to hold the knot in place. Continue by repeating step 3.

6 Work your way around the hoop, adding in new stems until the chandelier is complete.

7   Once you have reached the beginning knot,
    take the end of the stems of your final knot
    and carefully thread them into the stems of the
    original knot. If this feels insecure or stems are
    too fleshy to push through, then this last part
    can be secured with a length of wire.

8   Attach the ribbon in three equal placements
    around the hoop, looping them together at the
    top. The hoop should hang straight horizontally
    when it's in place, so adjust the position of
    the ribbons until it does so.

9   Hang out to dry and admire your finished
    buttercup chandelier.

Living Wreath

Many moons ago when I first left my corporate job, a sweet seedling of an idea forming in my mind as to how I may go on to make a living, I threw myself into learning all I could about growing flowers. I started volunteering with a good friend, Tracey, who ran a flower farm, and spent hours each week helping her get her season off the ground, sowing seeds, pricking out and planting. The winter was a cold one, yet mornings spent in her polytunnel felt like the purest, most enjoyable time of my life. Just to be away from my laptop, surrounded by all the hope that growing flowers from seeds can bring, was the perfect tonic for my weary heart.

Occasionally we would stop and play with the flowers, and one spring afternoon we gathered the ingredients for a living wreath. Working with ivy vine bases, wrapped in moss from the farm floor, I built my first living wreath. Delicate bulbs of muscari were interwoven with honesty seedpods and viburnum blossoms to create the most beautiful of wreaths, reminiscent of nature in late spring. What I loved about these wreaths we created was not only the aesthetic, but also that working with bulbs and small plants means that there is very little waste as the bulbs and plants can later be planted out into a pot on a windowsill or in your garden once they have finished flowering.

I build these wreaths on a moss base, which helps to retain water in the bulbs and plants that are carefully nestled in among the foliage and blossoms. The bulbs and plants themselves will last longer than the blossom, which can be lifted out when it begins to wilt or – if preferred – left to dry in situ. Some blossoms dry beautifully, including forsythia and double cherry blossoms, so you may be happy leaving those in place even when they have begun to go over. Spring foliage can be a bit tricky to work with: the fresh green growth wilts quickly as it's so full of fleshy, juicy life, but if we remember that this make is temporary, then we can make peace with the fleeting beauty of some of its elements. To create a wreath with slightly more longevity, consider using evergreens such as camellias, viburnum or bay.

Seek out extra twigs and interesting bits to add a final flourish and interest. Catkins from silver birch and the flowers of pussy willow are beautiful additions. Preserved seedheads from the previous season can also bring softness and lift the wreaths: adding ethereal seedheads of honesty will sparkle in among the lush new green growth and grasses.

These wreaths look beautiful on a front door and will fare better outside, where the roots of the plants can keep cool and absorb moisture from the air. A regular misting will help avert wilting, and if it's a very dry spring I will often submerge my wreath in a bucket of water, refilling the moss which keeps the plants watered. At some point, maybe in a month or two, the flowers will go over and the wreath will need to be taken down. The wreath base can be reused if it's not too damp, and the moss returned to the garden.

Gather

- ~ A moss wreath base
- ~ Tiny flowering plants such as violas, primroses and hellebores
- ~ Bulbs in bud: my favourites include muscari and miniature narcissi. Aim for flowers that have longevity, avoiding bulbs that have a short flowering time, such as crocuses
- ~ Extra flowers and foliage, such as the narcissi and alamancia foliage used here: I used these to poke into the moss to fill gaps. They won't last as long as the bulbs, and can be taken out and replaced when they begin to wilt
- ~ Moss: I gather mine from our garden floor, but there are sustainable suppliers available
- ~ Florist wire

Method

1 Working with a vine wreath base, wrap layers of moss around the vines to cover them completely, tying in place with a length of twine, or if you prefer wire.

2 Using your fingers or a stick, create small pockets within the moss to nestle larger plants such as primroses in. Carefully place the primroses in these little pockets, keeping some soil around the roots of the plants to ensure they are nourished and their roots won't dry out. Wrap the wire around the plant and the moss base to secure them together.

3 Next add in the bulbs. I like to leave the bulbs exposed as I adore their structural shapes, although they won't last as long if you decide to do this. Alternatively, tuck them into the moss surrounded by a layer of compost in the same way you added in the plants. When leaving the bulbs exposed, wrap the wire carefully around the top where the stem meets

the bulb and then secure to the wreath base by wiring them together.

4   From a design perspective, I like to cluster similar flowers together, much as they would appear in the wild; nestle 2–3 primroses in one place, and do similarly with the bulbs.

5   Once your living plants are in place, carefully add in the flower and foliage stems. Here I have clustered together a few stems of sweet-smelling narcissi by making a little bunch held together with wire and carefully feeding it into the moss base. Dot foliage around the flowers to add interest.

6   Keep going until the wreath looks full and abundant, appreciating that some of the moss will remain exposed as it is part of the beautiful design.

7   Secure a loop of wire from the top of the wreath base from which to hang it.

8   Once the plants and bulbs begin to wane, simply dismantle the wreath and plant them out in the garden for next spring. The moss wreath base can be saved and reused.

These wreaths are best hung on a front door outside, where they will benefit from the spring damp and rains. They will dry out quickly if positioned in the house. Regular misting and submerging in a bucket of water is the best way to keep the plants looking fresh, and with regular care they should last for at least a month, with the flowers and foliage requiring a refresh every now and then.

Nature as a Creative Medium

Discovering nature as my creative space and medium has gifted me a flexibility, forgiveness and freedom that I haven't experienced in years. After so long spent in stifling office-based roles where I felt lost, suffocated by self-doubt and full of anxiety, this new creative home feels deeply liberating.

Here, there are no rights or wrongs, no rules or limitations. Unlike manmade structures or conventional art forms, nature operates on its own terms, following its continuous cycle of growth, decay and renewal. This absence of judgement – something that once stifled me – has enabled me to experiment freely, to embrace failures as integral parts of the process rather than problems that must be solved or sources of shame. When working with nature, we must learn to be guided by her. If a stem naturally bends in a certain direction, forcing it otherwise risks breaking it. I've learned to embrace this and respond intuitively to the flowers I work with, to go with their flow rather than fight against them.

Engaging with nature in this way often requires surrendering control; allowing the uncertainty of the creative process to take place can often feel like we are a bystander just watching. I feel the same way when I garden; it's a constant battle to try to tame the way things grow, and we instead find harmony when working in tandem with nature to create spaces where both of us thrive.

These are some of the things I love about the use of nature as a creative medium:

— *Unlimited inspiration:* nature provides us with an inexhaustible source of inspiration to work with. From the intricate seedheads of wild carrot to the vibrant hues of strawflowers and the papery petals of ranunculus, there is always something to be found to ignite the imagination.

— *Anything goes:* my focus in this book is mainly flowers and foliage, but there are so many other objects to be found that we can add to our creations. Feathers, shells, abandoned bird's nests – all offer the opportunity to use materials that reflect the essence of the natural world.

— *The seasons:* nature's ever-changing landscape allows us to explore new and exciting combinations of materials with each month that dawns. This expands our creativity and keeps us on our creative toes as we shift from one season to another, exploring each one's colour palette, textures, shapes and structures.

— *Mindfulness:* I find solace and peace in working with nature. Whether it's sowing a seed, harvesting a flower or weaving stems together. Full immersion into the beauty of the natural world and the act of working with my hands helps to calm me and settle my emotions.

— *Connection:* I have been known to continue my creative practices when on holiday or visiting friends and family. Taking a few moments to explore my surroundings, selecting a few stems here and there to bring together in a display, helps me connect with where I am. At home I do this on a daily basis, so it's nice to take the practice away with me to foster a deeper connection to the places I visit.

— *Awe:* nature has provided me with more moments of awe than anything else in this world. Whether walking through the mountains in Spain, studying the intricacies of a spider web coated in Autumn dew or growing the most perfect of flowers, it is incredible. Awe is a magical feeling, one that can help to shift our perspectives, soothe our souls and fill our heads with dreams and possibilities.

Forcing Blossom Branches

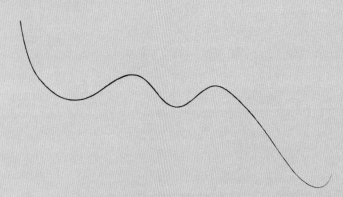

When I was in my early thirties, shortly after my eldest son arrived, I was transferred to the Netherlands for work. This period of time, living in a 600-year-old house in one of the most beautiful cities in the world, really shaped how I interacted with the natural world. It was the first time I had lived in a city, and I became fascinated with how the Dutch brought nature into their homes. There were also the most amazing flower markets on my doorstep, and these two things combined opened my eyes to the ways in which we can display and play with flowers.

I vividly remember the first time I discovered forcing branches for indoor blossom. It was a Saturday morning, and we had been to the market to buy food for the week. I had baby Henry strapped to my back, and as we walked past my favourite flower stall I saw huge branches of magnolias at cracked bud stage for sale. They were sitting alongside arching stems of blossom and my heart skipped a beat. I took the magnolia home and watched over the coming days as they slowly but surely opened into the most incredible blooms. Each flower was perfect in its make-up, looking resplendent. It felt like magic.

Nature can be so fleeting, particularly in early spring when the delicate blossoms are emerging, but we are still at the mercy of the weather; a late frost can wipe out magnolias in a single night, scorching their fleshy pink blooms and tinging them brown. And with the blossoms, a late passing storm can whip away their delicate petals leaving them strewn across the damp ground. To say my heart has been broken by years when the weather hasn't been kind is no exaggeration. So I always ensure I bring in a branch or two throughout the season to enjoy their beauty, unscathed by the weather outside. The year of writing this book has been a particularly good year for magnolia trees; with one of the wettest and mildest winters, they have been putting on the best show I can remember.

Most blossoms can be forced in this way, from magnolia to those that we may find in hedgerows, such as forsythia and hawthorn. When cutting stems for forcing, we are looking for those in cracked bud stage. If they are cut too early then the buds will not go on to flower, and if we leave it too late then the petals will shed before you get them back to the house. It can take a little time to get so you can judge the best stage, so don't be disheartened if it doesn't work the first time.

Choosing the right stem is important and you should keep in mind the vessel you plan to showcase your branches in. For large vessels I like to choose branches that have stature and a flowing structure, so they almost replicate a tree when in the vase, reaching up and then arching over. For smaller vessels such as bud vases, it can be lovely to cut just a few simple stems with the most flowers on them for displaying along a table or a mantelpiece.

Gather

~ A beautiful, stand-out vessel: those
   with a slightly nipped-in neck are best
~ Sharp, clean snips
~ Branches of cracked bud blossom

FAVOURITE BRANCHES TO FORCE FOR BLOSSOM

Magnolia
Forsythia
Crab apple
Cherry blossom
Mock orange
Flowering quince
Blackthorn

Method

1 Select your branch and remove it from the tree by making a clean cut with a sharp pair of snips. As with all flowers being cut for display, it helps to leave the branch to condition overnight in a cool, dark place.

2 Knowing when to cut the branch is critical, and it's rarely at the same time each year, particularly with the fluctuating weather due to climate change. It pays to keep a close eye on those you have selected for cutting. Look out for the swelling flower buds, and when one or two are just beginning to open (cracked bud stage) they are ready to be cut.

3 It's important to allow the branches to absorb as much water as possible when they are being displayed, and a trick I learnt while in Amsterdam is to cut the stems on a diagonal and then cut a slit up the stem in the middle.

This opens up the pores in the stem to absorb more water. Do this after the branch has been cut from the tree and after conditioning.

4 If you are working with particularly big branches, then some support may be required in the vessel. I find chicken wire works really well, as can a few carefully positioned rocks: both work better if you have chosen a ceramic vessel rather than glass.

5 Heat and sunlight will make the blossoms bloom faster, so choose where you're going to place your display carefully. The magnolia here has been placed in a dark corner of my living room, where the creamy white blossoms contrast against the grey and where the sunlight won't blow the flowers open too quickly.

Abundance

3

As spring fades to make room for the lush embrace of summer, anticipation fills the air.

We yearn for warmth and abundant sunlight, where the sun graces us with its presence from early morning until late into the evening. However, in the UK, dreams of basking in the heat aren't always fulfilled. Despite the extended daylight hours, the elusive warmth we long for can sometimes evade us. After all, we're just a small island at the mercy of an unpredictable and ever-changing jet stream.

Regardless of whether the weather cooperates, summer arrives in a burst of abundance. Nature proudly displays the fruits of her labour and our hard work, filling the garden with a symphony of life. Bees and hoverflies buzz busily from flower to flower, indulging in the sweet nectar offered so generously. Butterflies flit through wildflower meadows in a fleeting moment of beauty before they drift away.

I wish I could bottle the smell of summer, a symphony of green grass, zesty citrus and the heady perfume of roses, sweet peas and honeysuckle. I breathe it all in every day while walking in the garden at dawn, greeted by the sunrise painting the sky in hues of gold and pink. On my favourite mornings I wake early, hopping on my bike while the house sleeps, letting the hens out of their coop before I go. At this time of year it's harder to catch the sunrise, it's so early, but when I make it my reward is to step into the silky soft seawater before the crowds arrive, and it's one of the best ways to start the day. When the conditions are just right, the water dazzles in turquoise and emerald, the sunlight playing across the waves like a dance. The water is warmer now, and swimming is leisurely and comfortable.

Quiet joy

The transition into summer brings with it a welcome sense of tranquillity. The canopies of trees have reached their full glory, and the fledgling birds have bravely flown their nests. In the garden, the urgency of spring planting gives way to a more leisurely pace. Once the summer solstice has passed, signalling the peak of sunlight, the days begin to gradually shorten, bringing a shift in focus. While the garden continues to thrive, my attention turns to maintenance; unruly growth threatens to overtake the space, everything wants to expand outwards, and those plants I didn't quite manage to stake begin to droop towards the earth, their stems heavy with flowers and seedheads.

My evenings are spent walking up and down the allotment with watering cans, making sure to keep things watered and fed during this time of growth and expanse. As summer progresses, there's a quiet joy in simply being outside, the warmth providing comfort and ease. Long evenings are spent gathered around the fire, nestled among the wildflowers in moments of respite and celebration. It's a time to reflect on all that has been accomplished and relish the abundance of the season.

I'm cutting flowers in much larger quantities now for drying, and my studio begins to fill up once again. Cutting flowers is a task I find bittersweet, as taking flowers away can somehow feel like a betrayal of the garden's beauty. But I remind myself that most of the flowers I select are already fully bloomed, having generously offered their pollen and nectar to bees and butterflies. In fact, many plants benefit from regular cutting, stimulating further growth and blooms. Among the plants that are reaching their peak, umbellifers stand out, their delicate flower heads beginning to set seed. I trim them down to the ground, not only for their visual appeal but also for their potential in larger installations. Both the flower heads and seedheads are carefully dried, ready to be incorporated into future projects.

Summer brings with it a natural slowdown in my work, and I welcome it with open arms, embracing the opportunity to rest and recharge. While this ebb and flow of activity within my work was never part of the plan, I relish the long, lazy days stretching out before me. I savour every moment with my boys, as if this might be the last summer that they swing on rope swings with me and hold my hand tightly as we head out on walks. Mornings become a peaceful ritual of sipping hot water and lemon on the front decking, accompanied only by the soft birdsong. I steal moments of relaxation in the hammock beneath our copper beech tree, basking in the dappled sunlight. As a family, we embark on adventures, spending weeks camping and immersing ourselves in nature, away from the bustle of daily life.

Summer's harvest

Summer is when the allotment really comes into its own and I spend many evenings on the land, harvesting, weeding and tidying until the sun sets. Then it's time to cycle the long, steep journey home, collapsing into bed in an exhausted but happy heap, my basket laden with the season's bounty. I spend a lot of time working on my own, and so time spent on the allotment counters this. There's always someone to chat to, offering company and conversation about the growing season.

Summer also offers a rare opportunity to share the allotment with my family. Though the boys may need a bit of coaxing to join me, the promise of digging up potatoes and picking fresh mangetout is usually enough to entice them. Watching their faces light up as they pluck peas straight from the pods or unearth the biggest potato delights both me and them. And there's nothing quite like enjoying a meal made from our own harvest.

In August, there's a subtle shift in the air that heralds the arrival of autumn. It's not yet cold, but there's a crispness to the morning breeze, and a thin veil of mist hangs over the fields, adorning the intricate spiderwebs with glistening dew. As I wander through the wildflower patch, I notice more seedheads than blooms, a sign that it's time to harvest.

The perennial beds, once lush and vibrant, now droop under the weight of heavy summer rains, signalling the beginning of the end of their season. Before autumn's chill sets in, I set about gathering seeds from my garden. Earlier in the year, I marked the finest stems with red ribbons, allowing them to mature and set seed for the next season. Now I carefully cover each seedhead with a paper bag, snipping it off and collecting the seeds inside. I lay them out to dry in the studio before storing them away in a cool, dark place.

These rituals feel like second nature to me, a comforting routine that reconnects me with the rhythms of the seasons. Each task is like greeting an old friend, a familiar and cherished part of my journey through the year. In the lanes, the familiar hum of tractors signals the start of verge-cutting season. With a sense of urgency, I venture out, hoping to gather any remaining seedheads before they're lost to the blades. My keen eye spots the most promising stems, and I make mental notes to return before the farmers do their work. Back in the studio, it's a delightful chaos of drying stems, occupying every spare space. As I navigate through this sea of abundance, I can't help but marvel at all that I've grown and nurtured throughout the year.

Wildflower
Wreath

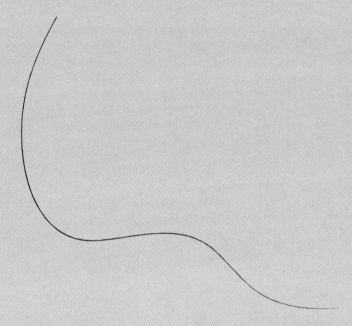

My wildflower meadow in the garden is at its peak from early to midsummer. During this time it is bursting with grasses that are just beginning to fade, with the lush purple heads of knapweed starting to flush and swathes of hawkweed shining bright yellow in the morning sun before releasing their fluffy seedpods as the sun sets later in the day. Butterflies and hoverflies flit from flower to flower, and the crickets and grasshoppers begin to make themselves known, a quiet hum that builds as the season progresses. Teasels are standing tall and statuesque at the rambling edges of our garden, bright green for now, with their purple top hats: in my opinion this is the perfect time to pick them, but many people prefer to wait until they are golden brown later in the summer.

This wreath is a celebration of the wildness of my garden in the height of the summer. Most of the plants I have selected could be considered weeds by others and dismissed in favour of blooms from their gardens or the shops, but look at the beauty that can be created by choosing to work with less-favoured flowers. I can often get overwhelmed with our wild and natural space at this time of year: while I love the wildness, there is a small part of me that fears what could be perceived as mess and yearns for a neat and tidy town garden like we had before we moved here. But taking the time to appreciate the delicate beauty of what can be found within the wildflower meadow and garden edges emphasises how important it is that we don't always tidy up the edges and mow the lawn.

If you aren't growing or don't have access to a garden and want to create a seasonal wreath such as this, then it can still be achieved. Walk the hedgerows or verges of woodlands and take a peek at all that is growing there. I promise that you will be able to find enough stems to weave together a wreath of your own. Remember the rules of foraging (read about this on page 18) before setting out. You can also use dried materials to create this wreath following the same technique outlined in the method.

Gather

- ~ Vines for the wreath base: I have used honeysuckle here
- ~ Wildflowers, grasses and seedheads of your choosing: I used cocksfoot, pennycress, teasels, knapweed, orlaya seedheads and hawkweed seedheads
- ~ String or twine
- ~ Length of ribbon

Method

1   Gently tease the vine into a circle: the size is your choice, but ensure it works for the stems you have selected. The wreath base used here is approximately 40 cm (16 in), which was needed as many of the stems were fairly long when cut from the meadow.

2   Attach the twine to the wreath base on one side. I have worked from left to right, going anti-clockwise, simply because that feels best for me, but if it flows more easily for you to work clockwise starting on the righthand side then go for it.

3   Prepare the stems by stripping any excess leaves from the length of stem below the main flower and cutting to a good length to work with. Lay the flowers out on a bench or table, grouped together for ease of selecting when building the wreath.

4   Begin by placing some chosen flowers over the top of where the string has been secured to the wreath base, ensuring that the stems flow in the direction of the base. I like to fan the stems out to build a full wreath with flowers that extend both outwards and inwards.

5   Wrap the twine around the stems a couple of times to secure them in place and continue to hold the twine with your left or right hand, depending upon which way you are building the wreath, to keep the stems and twine securely in place.

6   With your spare hand, layer more flowers over the existing stems, working in a criss-cross motion using various lengths of stems to build up the wreath from all sides. Once you have added in a few stems, secure in place with a couple of wraps of twine.

7   Continue in this way until approximately half the wreath has been covered with flowers and seeds. Loop the twine around your forefinger and thread the loose end through the loop and pull it tight. This can be repeated several times to ensure the stems are held in position.

8   If you see that there are any gaps in the wreath, add in more stems by gently teasing them in among the existing ones, ensuring resistance can be felt – this means that the stem will be positioned securely and won't fall out.

9   Finish with a sturdy ribbon to complement the size of the wreath.

Garden Meadow Box

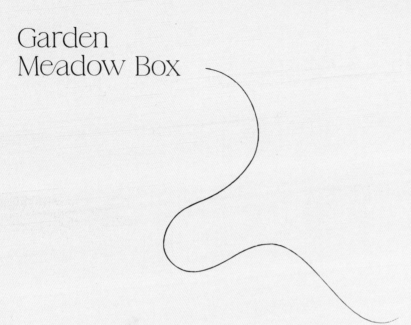

Part of the process of creating with flowers that I love most is reproducing scenes from nature as pieces of art. This meadow box captures the fleeting beauty of the height of summer using sand-dried flowers (see page 26 for information on how to do this) to make a display that can be lovingly preserved and enjoyed for many months.

Many of the flowers featured here are hard to dry in other ways. Flowers such as poppies and cosmos, when carefully dried in sand, give the illusion of still being fresh; while retaining their shape they take on a translucent quality, ethereal and ephemeral.

You can create meadow box scenes using fresh flowers as well as dried. For a display using fresh flowers, use a container that can hold water and fill it before placing in the stems; adding moss will hold the water for extra moisture, ensuring fresh flowers last for a good week or so. The container in this project is an old vintage poultry feeder that I picked up at a car boot sale (yard sale) when I fell in love with its patinaed edges. You can find concrete troughs to purchase online, or seek out a long, thin vessel that will allow you to build up a front-facing shallow display of flowers.

When selecting flowers and other materials, spend some time exploring how the stems combine in the wild before cutting or drying them. All the flowers for this display were cut from the borders in front of my house, and when pieced together form a snapshot of these – a sweet reflection of the outside when positioned in my living room.

I've previously created a meadow scene very similar to this using dried grasses, buttercups and oxeye daisies along with stems of sorrel, so delicate in its beauty. It's good to consider different shapes and sizes of flowers to combine. Here, the tall seedheads of cephalaria gigantea reach high above the other flowers in the mix in much the same way as they do in my borders. Lower down we have the poppies, oxeye daisies intermingled with aquilegia 'yellow queen', and dainty nigella and orlaya filling the gaps below near the front of the trough. I have maintained a level of negative space so as not to overcrowd the flowers and to allow each stem space to breathe: this is something I find particularly hard to replicate when gardening, as I am the type of grower that tries to squeeze everything into the tiniest space, when there is so much to be said for giving each plant or stem the room it needs to flourish, whether in the garden or in our art.

Gather

~ Selection of sand-dried flowers in various shapes, sizes and colours: I have used poppies, aquilegia, oxeye daisies, nigella, orlaya, cephalaria gigantea and trifolium ochroleucon
~ Shallow, long and thin vessel
~ Chicken wire
~ Moss

Method

1 Using a set of pliers, carefully cut the chicken wire into a strip that can be inserted into the cavity of the vessel, allowing for a couple of folds along the way to give the stems plenty to balance onto.

2 Push the chicken wire down into the vessel, ensuring that it can't be seen from the top edge of the vessel.

3 Cover the chicken wire with a layer of moss pushed down on top of the chicken wire. The moss is not only there for aesthetics, but also to help hold the stems in a secure position.

4 Add in your strongest stems first to build a frame within which the more delicate stems can be positioned. Here, I began by adding in the cephalaria and trifolium at various organic intervals along the vessel: these were for the most part positioned towards the back of the vessel, allowing space at the front for the smaller, more delicate stems.

5 Once these sturdier stems are in position, slowly build up the display by layering with the other flowers stems. Consider if the display is going to be visible from both the front and the back, as this will impact where the flowers are positioned.

6 This display was designed to be positioned against a wall, so I regularly took time to step away from the vessel to observe the placement of flowers from afar and at eye level. Pay attention to negative space and also to the natural clustering of flowers heads, mirroring the way in which plants grow in the wild.

Smudge Sticks

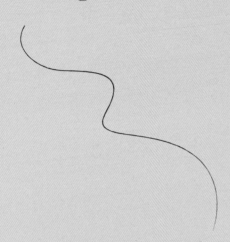

After attending retreats and healing workshops over the last couple of years, I became a little bit obsessed with smudge sticks (used in rituals and ceremonies), and began to wonder whether I could make my own. I had seen practitioners burn white sage and palo santo (neither of which I recommend using, as they are sourced from far away and often include no information as to how they have been sourced), and I began experimenting with plant materials I had growing in and around my garden.

While herbal smudge sticks have surged in popularity in recent years, they have been used for years and years in smudging ceremonies often in conjunction with spiritual cleansing. This historical aspect explains why it became important that herbs and flowers native to southeast Mexico and South America were traditionally included in smudge sticks. The smudge sticks here are a celebration of local flora, offering a chance to step outside and pluck leaves, flower heads and stems to bind together for burning. It's a wonderful way to incorporate herbs and flowers that have meaning, and there are lots of resources giving information on this topic on the internet if you want to go down that rabbit hole, but it's not completely necessary.

The best time to collect herbs and flowers for smudge sticks is in the summer. I made these in mid-July when we had experienced endless amounts of rain, so not the ideal time for picking. But out I went with my basket and, dodging the showers, I managed to find roses, sage, lavender, chamomile, bay leaves, thyme, mullein leaves and yarrow. I would advise against buying-in dried flowers and herbs to create your smudge sticks. Not only is the selecting and picking part of the ritual, it's also crucial we can be sure that plant materials we are going to burn are in their purest form; we cannot know what processes bought-in dried flowers have been through before they reach us.

The herbs and plants you put in the smudge stick are the important components when it comes to perfume and purpose. For the most part flowers are there for the visual aesthetic (apart from chamomile and lavender, which also offer scent and meaning); they carry with them energy that will be released when the smudge stick is burnt but it's the herbs that will do the most work. To determine whether a plant material is good for using in a smudge stick, dry a small amount and touch a flame to it to see how it burns and what smell it gives off. I would only ever select flowers and plants that I know can be eaten or used medicinally, avoiding all plants that could be toxic. Common sense is vitally important here.

Gather

- ~ Fresh herbs (8–10 per smudge stick)
- ~ Flower petals for decoration
- ~ Snips
- ~ Natural twine

Smudge sticks can be made using both fresh and dried materials. If you're using fresh then they will need to be hung out to dry for a good few weeks to ensure they are ready to be burnt.

Method

1   Choose your sprigs for each bundle; if making multiple bundles then gather them together in small piles. Make sure the stems are all facing the same direction as it is the leaf and flower end you will begin to burn from.

2   If you are using fresh herbs and flowers, remember that your smudge sticks will shrink as they dry so it's worth packing them out nicely to create generous bunches.

3   Cut a length of natural twine that is roughly five times the length of the stick.

4   Working at the base of the bundle, wrap the twine around the stems very tightly and then tie it off in a knot using the two ends of twine.

5   Wrap your twine up and around the stems, leaves and flowers, spiralling around the bundle as you go, ensuring that the twine is pulled nice and taut when doing so.

6   Once you've reached the top, head back down with the twine, cross-crossing over the existing wraps to create a nicely bound aesthetic.

7   Circle around the base once again and then tie off the twine.

8   Lay your bunches out to dry for 2–3 weeks in a warm space. You can check whether they are ready to be burnt by breaking a stalk off; if it snaps off easily, then you're good to go.

Summer Floral Weaving

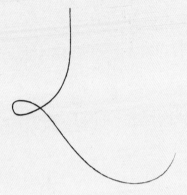

I'm forever seeking out opportunities to work with my hands in the evenings when I finally retreat indoors, looking for projects and crafts that I can do in the house. While I've tried many different creative pursuits in the past, including knitting and embroidery, they just haven't stuck. I struggle with anything that requires numbers, planning and order – my brain goes into meltdown. Weaving as demonstrated here is freeing: there are no patterns to follow, no numbers to count, just a gentle, meditative flow of bringing together natural fabrics and dried flower stems.

These weavings reflect the seasons and our individual styles and creativity. They can be created throughout the year, with the best times being summer and autumn when the flowers and seedheads are abundant, but they can look just as striking created in winter using lichen-covered twigs and structural stems. I've even seen examples of weavings that incorporate feathers and other natural materials, and I plan to create a weaving with dried seaweed from the beaches here in Devon. Use your imagination and whatever you have to hand.

Weavings – whether of the type that bring together fabrics and plant materials or the more traditional complex weavings – bring texture and softness into the home. They can be large-scale or smaller, more delicate versions, such as the one shown here.

I created this weaving frame out of an old picture frame (with the glass removed), with small tacks hammered into the top and bottom from which to loop the base thread. I would urge you to use what is to hand rather than buying anything new. There are all sorts of weaving tools and equipment available to buy, but they're really not necessary when making something this simple. Another option is to make a frame out of pieces of wood or sticks in a rectangle or square, nailed or pulled together with twine. The thread can then be looped over the frame itself, doing away with the need to use nails and allowing for the frame itself to become part of the piece.

When selecting plant materials to use for the weaving, I find it best to focus on those with sturdy stems as you will be threading them in and out of the weave. Stems that are too delicate can be tricky to work with, and it's the same with flowers that are too fragile. I originally used buttercups in this design, but found the delicate heads and stems got caught up in my threads as I was working. It is possible to work with flowers and seedheads when they are in their fresh form, as long as the botanicals selected are of the woodier stemmed variety; anything too fleshy may be damaged as you work with them.

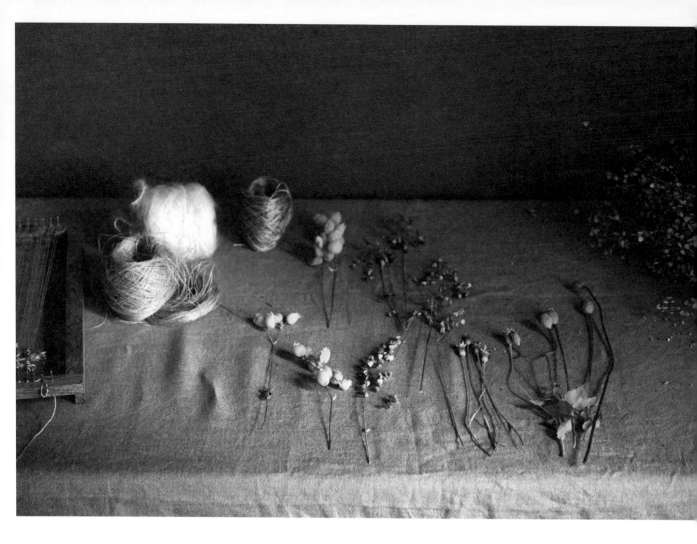

Gather

- ∼ Variety of different plant materials:
  consider the colour palette and
  the different shapes and textures
  of the plant materials. I've worked
  with xeranthemum annuum flower
  heads, poppy seedheads, briza media
  seedheads and silene seedheads
- ∼ Wooden frame
- ∼ Nails (if following the technique shown
  on these pages)
- ∼ Natural threads and twines in colours
  that complement your plant materials.
  Pay attention to different textures of
  threads, too: here I have used varying
  thicknesses as well as some with a
  bit of fluff

Method

1 Begin by creating your base structure. In this design I looped my chosen thread up and around each of the nails that I hammered into the picture frame. If you have chosen to make a frame out of sticks or twigs and are not using nails, then you can simply wrap your thread around the frame from top to bottom. The placement of nails dictated the number of loops I made; however this is something that can be adapted depending upon the desired size of your weaving.

2 Secure both ends of the thread and ensure that the strands of thread are tight on the frame.

3 To begin the weave, start with a length of one of your chosen threads: this is all about personal choice and what looks good to you, but I do encourage you to start with thread as this helps with the structure. Weave your thread through the upright strands of thread.

We are creating a solid base-weave here as this is what will hold the piece together, so weave up and down each alternate strand of thread.

4 When you reach the end, head back in the opposite direction until 4–6 lines have been woven. Gently tease all the weaves together by pushing down with your fingers, ensuring that you leave a good couple of centimetres (about an inch) of the vertical strands of thread clear at the bottom for knotting later.

5 The next stage is to either add more lines of woven thread, perhaps choosing a different weave, thickness or colour to contrast or complement, or to add one of your selected plant materials. When adding in the stems of flowers or seedheads, they can be threaded through two or three of the strands, pushing them carefully down towards your woven thread to ensure they are in position tightly.

6   Build up the line of flowers or seedheads by weaving them across the line of weave; this will mean cutting down stems to be a little shorter to allow you to weave flower heads in towards the centre.

7   Continue to build up the weave, alternating plant materials with the threads. Remember that it is the threads that will help to hold all the pieces in position.

8   Once you reach the end of the weave – ensuring that you leave enough space in the top section of thread strands clear to tie knots (about 5 cm [2 in] should suffice) – finish with a final few lines of thread. Again, this just helps to hold everything in position.

9   Tidy up any ends of thread by tying them in knots or cutting any loose ends off after tucking them safely into the reverse of the weave.

10 This next part applies to when you're working with a nailed frame like that shown here. If you have chosen to create your own frame, your weave is now complete and can be hung. If you're working with a frame and nails, weave a thin wooden twig or stake in between each of the loops of thread on both the top and the bottom. We will be cutting the threads and tying them in knots around the stick, so make sure that the way the stick is woven into the thread will allow for this to happen.

11 Once the sticks are secure at the top and the bottom, cut the threads and tie each loop that has been cut into a knot at the top of the stick. This should hold the threads and weaves in place.

12 Take a length of your thread and tie a loop from either side of the top of the weaving for hanging.

Hapa Zome

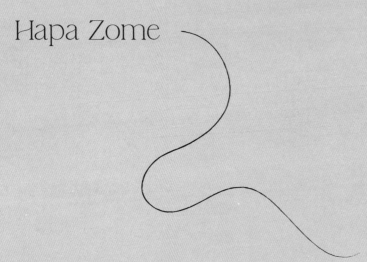

Petal printing, or 'hapa zome', is an ancient Japanese printing technique that offers a simple yet incredibly effective way of imprinting the fleeting beauty of flowers and leaves onto fabric. It feels a little like magic and happens so instantaneously that it's hard to stop once you get going.

The flower imprints will fade over time, lightening up and altering in appearance, and won't survive the wash unless you take the time to mordant the fabric, but even then I find they do lose their vibrancy over time and repeated washes. This is maybe because the types of flowers I have used to imprint perhaps don't have the depth of dye required to last forever. However, I don't mind this. For me it's another example of the fragility and fleeting nature of flowers and plants.

I found this old dress while clearing out my closet and decided to give it a revamp by playing around with petals and shapes created by printing violas and pansies over the front. I love the results and, while I know they won't last, it's a beautiful way to brighten up what is otherwise a simple summer dress. The dress's fabric is linen, which tends to work well as a fabric to print on; the tight weave supports the flower's shape and gives a true representation of the flowers. This technique can also be used on silk; I find when petal printing on silk that the colours tend to run, but this gives a sort of watercolour effect and is absolutely stunning. You could also try this technique on recycled paper or natural paper, any surface that has some roughness that allows the colour to permeate.

Violas and pansies are a must-have in my garden throughout most of the year and were used to create the pressings on this dress. They are true cut-and-come-again flowers (which means the more you cut their blooms, the more flowers they will push out) which brighten our darker days and fill our lighter days with joy. The range of colours and styles is dazzling, and amazingly, they are also edible – which is even more reason to grow them: add them to salads and desserts at your summer parties. If you are unable to grow them yourself there are plenty of online suppliers selling them as edible flowers, which is a great way to obtain them if you want to have a go at petal printing.

When selecting flowers or leaves to work with, choose those with brighter petals and colours as these will leave the strongest imprints on your fabric or paper. It's a good idea to practise first on a scrap piece of fabric or paper to make sure that the combinations work well together. While the dress design here mainly uses violas and pansies, there are so many beautiful and inspiring combinations that can be created using all sorts of plant materials.

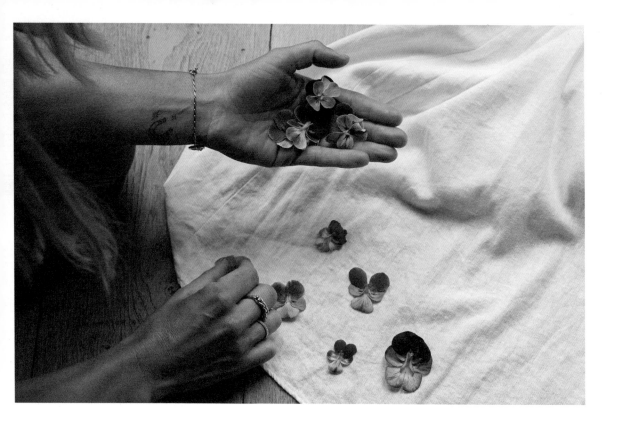

A FEW OF MY FAVOURITES

Cosmos
Cornflowers
Roses
Buddleia
Marigolds
Chrysanthemums

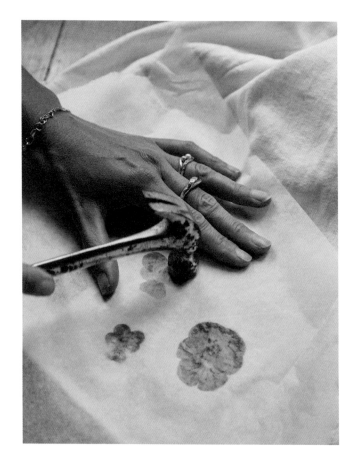

Gather

- ~ Wax paper
- ~ Fabric or paper of your choice
- ~ A good number of flower heads and leaves of your choice
- ~ A mallet or hammer
- ~ Tweezers

Method

1 Lay your fabric or paper out on a hard surface. I have found that my floor works best, because when I attempted to hammer onto my wooden kitchen table it wasn't quite sturdy enough.

2 Lay the flowers face down on the fabric or paper in your chosen pattern and position.

3 Place a layer of wax paper over the top of the flowers. I like to use wax paper because you can view the flowers through it, which helps to see if enough of the flowers have been hammered onto the fabric. If you can't get hold of wax paper, then another piece of fabric or sturdy paper will work well.

4 Using your hammer or mallet, carefully pound the back of the flowers through the paper or fabric, aiming to hammer all corners, edges and centre parts of the flowers to ensure complete imprinting of their faces.

5 The hammering should be light: too heavy and the flowers will turn to mush and lose their structure and appearance.

6 When you are happy that all the flowers have been imprinted, carefully lift the wax paper off, removing any residual petals or leaves by picking them off: tweezers can be useful here.

7 Hang the fabrics out to dry before brushing to remove any remaining petals.

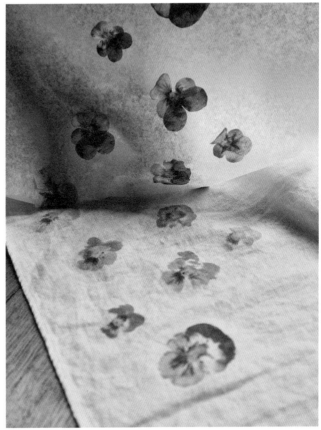

Nature Meditations

Stepping outside and immersing oneself in nature is one of the simplest ways to connect with the natural world. However, in our fast-paced lives, it can take practise to slow down and truly appreciate the beauty around us. Often we rush from one place to another without pausing to notice the wonders that are right on our doorsteps.

While connecting with nature does take time and practise, it is something that can be done in just a few minutes each day. And the impact can be profound. There have been many studies into the benefits of time spent in nature, and the results are clear: those who have a strong connection to nature are found to generally be happier and healthier, with time spent in nature providing tranquillity and joy and encouraging creativity. I've felt this acutely in my own life: if I'm struggling with a problem or beginning to feel myself slipping into a negative frame of mind, being outside – either gardening, walking or simply being – does wonders to lift me up and restore me.

Here are a few simple ways to step outside and truly immerse yourself in nature:

Remove distractions

If you're looking to deepen your connection with nature, one of the simplest yet most effective ways to start is by taking a walk, free from distractions. Our phones, in particular, can be constant companions that prevent us from being fully present in the moment. Leaving them behind when we walk (if you feel safe to do so) allows us to be more focused on and attentive to the natural world around us.

Barefoot walking

There are many benefits to walking barefoot outside, with our whole foot in contact with the earth. And while it can feel uncomfortable to begin with, it is surprising how gentle the ground feels. It's been shown that when our feet touch the ground it can help us to absorb antioxidants, helping us to sleep better as well as reducing inflammation. Walking barefoot feels incredible, too.

Last year I spent some time in the ancient woods of Dartmoor, and each morning I would wake and walk barefoot through the forest to reach the rushing ice-cold river. I was surprised by how much I enjoyed the feeling of mud squelching through my toes and how bouncy the expanses of intricate mosses were under the soles of my feet, caressing me as I tiptoed to my destination.

My favourite time to walk barefoot in the garden is first thing in the morning. I always wake early, before the rest of the house, and so those few moments spent outside leaning into the feelings that come up as I walk over grass and soil are important. If you don't have a garden then consider walking barefoot for a short while when you are next at your local park.

Nature noticing

A lot of what I share in this book is about noticing: noticing the changes in the seasons, the way plants grow and combine together, the way a flower fades over time. So much of my work and how I have evolved as a creative has involved me spending a lot of time noticing. This practice expands on the idea of noticing and encourages us to use all our senses to study a single object for a short period of time.

Head outside and choose an object in nature. If you're in a city this could be a tree in a park or a flower growing out of the pavement cracks. Deeper in the countryside you may choose a stream or meadow or a wildflower in the hedgerows. Focus on your chosen nature object and take a few minutes to really study it using all of your senses. Touch it, feeling the edges and the centre; notice if it is smooth or hard, delicate or sturdy. Lift it to your nose and breathe in its scent. Perhaps if you hold it close to your ear it makes a noise as the breeze flutters past.

Taking the time to really study your object in this way fosters a deeper connection to nature but can also be a fascinating exercise. How often do you pass things by without truly seeing them? When we slow down and study these incredible feats of nature we can see just how clever they really are.

Apricity bathing

Apricity is the feeling of the unexpected warmth of the winter sun on your skin. After days and weeks – and, in the case of this past winter, months – of darkness and cold, that first day the sun shines and you can feel the strength of her rays on your body is one of the best feelings in the world. This feeling of pure joy is enough to lift you up and fill your heart and mind with positivity, carrying you through the rest of winter and beyond. It is a feeling of hope and excitement, carrying a sliver of a remembrance of what's to come. On these days, which are so often fleeting, find the time (it doesn't have to be long, five minutes will suffice) to step outside and turn your face up to the sun. Find a comfortable seat and rest with your chin tilting upwards, eyes closed, and let the sun's rays stroke your skin and fuel your mind and body.

Solstice Flower
Crown

The summer solstice is such a powerful point in the meteorological calendar, and one that I always mark. Sunrise at this time of year is roughly around 5am, and my tradition since moving to the coast is to rise while the sky is just beginning to glow and cycle down to the beach for a swim with friends and other souls. For the last few years we have been graced with the most incredible skies and calm seas, and despite the early start I always feel so energised for the rest of the day. The power of the sun and of the community of people enjoying the warm seas is life-giving.

I have long dreamt of taking a trip to Sweden to celebrate 'midsommar' in the way only they know how. In the Nordic countries the sun barely sets at this midpoint of the year, and the occasion is marked by gatherings at summer houses and lakes, where flower crowns are worn and celebrations held. This project is entirely inspired by my dreams of visiting Sweden and is another example of living in the moment and appreciating what the land has to offer us at any given time.

This flower crown is made to be entirely compostable, but also designed to be created using fresh flowers that can be worn (and will withstand being out of water for a period of time) before being hung in the home to dry out on display, evolving into a dried flower wreath over time.

When selecting the materials to work with, I walked the garden and the allotment to see what was in bloom. The oxeye daisies were in abundance, and coupled with the verdant alchemilla mollis are the perfect combination. If you don't have these to hand then work with what you can find, considering the shapes and structures of your flowers when selecting them. I chose the alchemilla mollis to give the flower crown body while supporting the heads of the oxeye daisies.

Gather

- ～ Length of vine: I have used a thin length of Virginia creeper, but honeysuckle or hops would also work well
- ～ String or twine
- ～ Flowers: here I have used oxeye daisies and alchemilla mollis
- ～ Ribbon to finish

Method

1. Shape the vine into a circle, using your head as a guide for size. The vine should wrap around itself and stay in position by carefully manipulating the ends.
2. Attach your twine or string to the vine base in any position by wrapping it around the base a couple of times and securing in a double knot.
3. Gather a small posy of your chosen materials. Here I selected a stem of alchemilla mollis and a couple of stems of oxeye daisies. The size of the stems you work with is entirely up to you. If you prefer a delicate flower crown then cut your flowers into smaller sections, always ensuring you have a good length of stem to work with.
4. Place the posy by laying it on top of the outer edge of the vine base, positioned above where the string is affixed to the flower crown base, and wrap the string around the bottom part of the stems a couple of times to secure them in place.
5. Continuing in the same direction, add a few more flowers by laying the stems over the top of those already in place and securing with a couple of winds of twine.
6. Work your way around the base of the flower crown until roughly two thirds of the vine base is covered in flowers.
7. To finish, loop the twine around your finger, feeding the end through the loop under your finger and pulling tightly to secure. This can be done a couple of times for extra security. Snip off the end of the twine
8. If you have chosen to use a ribbon, wind this around the exposed base of the crown, meeting back in the middle and allowing the long ends of the ribbon to hang down freely.
9. Once the flower crown has been worn, hang it from a nail indoors to allow the flowers to dry out naturally over time.

Fading

4

Autumn, in all its breathtaking beauty, unfolds in a spectacular array of colours.

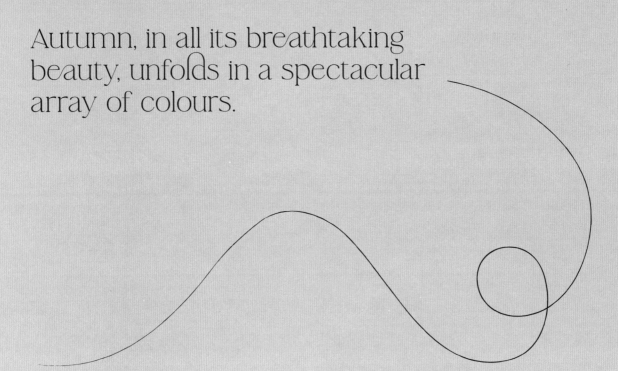

From first onset to final days, it takes us on a transformative journey through a kaleidoscope of hues, abundant harvests and the eventual unveiling of bare branches and damp earth. The transitions are nothing short of dramatic, marking a profound shift in the landscape and rhythms of the natural world. Autumn has always held a special place in my heart, and I think of it as 'my' season. Even before my work became so deeply intertwined with it, I have always favoured all that this season brings.

The beginning of autumn holds a familiar pattern for me since our move to Devon. As the boys return to school, calm settles over the house. It's become a tradition for me to mark the start of the season with a solitary swim in the sea, after bidding farewell to the boys as they embark on their new school year. With the departure of holidaymakers, the beach once again becomes my sanctuary. These moments of solitude are precious, especially after a bustling summer filled with the laughter and chatter of family life. Enveloped in the soothing embrace of the sea, under the gentle warmth of the lingering summer sun, I find myself replenished and ready to embrace the busy season ahead for my business.

Dusk and dawn – those transitions from day to night and vice versa – hold a special magic for me, especially during autumn. These moments are when I feel most alive creatively, whether I'm out photographing nature's beauty or tending the garden, harvesting flowers or planting seeds for the next year. As the long days of summer gradually give way to autumn, there's a subtle shift in the quality of light, a gentle dimming that offers welcome respite. It's a time of richness and abundance, with a bountiful harvest that feels like a reward for the year's hard work.

The world seems to exhale a collective sigh of relief as the year draws to a close. Hedges burst with ripening fruits – blackberries, sloes, holly berries, and elderberries – while flowers begin to set seed, preparing for the cycle of renewal in the coming year. In the garden and on the allotment, the flowers continue to bloom, albeit more slowly and with less vigour. Soon it will be time to cut back the spent annuals, although I often favour leaving them in place until early next year, providing nourishment and shelter for the birds and bees. Their silhouettes against the winter sky serve as a reminder of their past beauty and the promise of new life to come.

Gathering in

Surrounded by a lavish abundance of grasses, leaves and seedheads, I gather armfuls to bring back to the studio for drying. Many of these plants are already in the process of drying, their stems parched by the summer sun. Metal buckets overflow with umbellifers and wildflowers, each stem a testament to the beauty of the season. As I work, my mind teems with ideas for creative projects – installations, wreaths and more. I keep a close watch on the wild clematis creeping over the hedgerows, waiting for just the right moment to harvest it. If I wait too long, the fluffy green seedheads will turn and scatter in the wind as I pluck them free.

September marks a period of reflection for me. I delve into my daily journal, reviewing the successes and lessons learned from the growing season. Amid the hustle of harvest time, I also turn my gaze towards the future. Sowing hardy annuals early allows me to establish crops that will overwinter, giving me a jump-start on the next growing season. It often feels like there's never a moment to rest in the cycle of growth, but this constant momentum fills me with hope for what's ahead. Seed plucked fresh from the growing space always germinates brilliantly, and the greenhouse slowly begins to fill back up with seed trays and seedlings.

As the season progresses, I find myself yearning for the cosy comforts that accompany autumn. Though it's not yet cool enough to light the fire or indulge in our Sunday roast tradition, the anticipation builds with each passing day. I'm drawn to the woods, where I wander along windy lanes, my senses attuned to the signs of the changing season. Above me, the leaves begin their transformation, while below I keep a keen eye out for the first mushrooms peeking through the forest floor. My husband Ed joins in the hunt during his lunch breaks, filling his basket with woodland treasures. When the first heavy rains arrive, our efforts are rewarded with a harvest of penny buns and hedgehog mushrooms.

Autumnal display

In the autumn months, my focus shifts from studying trees for signs of blossom to observing their gradual fading. The copper beech in our back garden is always the first to shed its leaves, a slow process that culminates in a sudden flurry on stormy days, but it's the front garden that offers the most spectacular autumnal display. Trees are ablaze with colours that glow in the low sun, from the golden yellow of the gingko leaves to the ruby reds and burnt oranges of the acers. The towering beech trees transition from lush green to deep chestnut and coffee tones.

My work takes me across the UK, and I find joy in the long drives, particularly along the A303, one of the main routes in the West Country. The roadside trees undergo a breathtaking transformation, their once-green foliage becoming a riot of fiery colours. Shades of crimson, scarlet and golden amber paint a vibrant picture along the hills and valleys.

During this season, I keep a watchful eye on foliage and seedheads, knowing that many of the plant materials I harvest will be used in my winter projects. It's a delicate balance, knowing when to cut: too soon risks immaturity, while waiting too long risks damage from rain or frost. I rush out with my snips at the slightest hint of adverse weather, ensuring I gather the treasures of the hedgerows and garden before they're lost. Temptation is everywhere, from twisting vines stripped bare to lichen-covered branches fallen from old hawthorn trees. Each find holds the promise of future creations, feeding my creative thoughts and visions.

As the season draws to a close, storms begin to roll in and nature slowly reveals its bare bones. I step outside one morning to find that all the trees and shrubs, except for the tenacious young beeches, have shed their leaves. The ground is carpeted in a thick layer of leaves. I gather enough to make leaf mulch to nurture the soil of my beds and leave the rest on the ground to return to the earth.

The days have grown noticeably shorter now, with the shortest day of the year just a few weeks away. Despite the fading light, work is picking up pace as Christmas approaches. My thoughts are firmly centred on the holiday season, preparing for the festivities just around the corner

Harvest Wreath

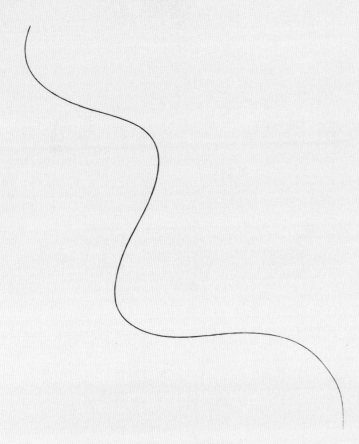

With the arrival of autumn comes a change in the colour palette outside our windows. Gone are the verdant greens of spring and early summer, replaced with burnt oranges and rusts and all the golden hues from spent grasses and seedheads. Our wildflower meadow is reaching the end of its season, but we hold off cutting it down until the goldfinches that flock to feast on the seeds have had their fill. Late flowers such as dainty Michaelmas daisies begin to bloom along the road verges and edges of my garden. The cosmos will flower their socks off until the first frost, alongside echinacea and eryngium, so beloved of the bees and butterflies.

This wreath is a celebration of autumn in all its finery, gathering all the flowers, colours and textures from this wonderful time of year. It's flamboyant and joyful, and ever so easy to put together. Because late summer and early autumn are such abundant times for flowers, it's worth checking out local florists and even supermarkets to seek out locally grown blooms to dry yourself at this time of year. Flowers that have been grown in the UK will state this on the packaging, and such beauties as sunflowers, China asters and chrysanthemums can all be bought fresh.

As the season shifts, my focus becomes the leaves on the trees, waiting for them to begin to turn from the heavy greens to rich tones that signify autumn proper has arrived. Gather armfuls of leaves on their branches and dry them flat, laid out in between sheets of cardboard to dry open rather than curling inwards. Some of my favourite leaves to dry at this time of year are copper beech, beech, silver birch and acers.

Gather

- ~ Dried flowers: I have used strawflowers, golden rod and Iona in this wreath
- ~ Dried foliage: I have used spindle leaves, hops and bracken
- ~ Seedheads
- ~ Wreath base: I purchased mine from an online craft store, to make your own use birch branches bound with binding wire

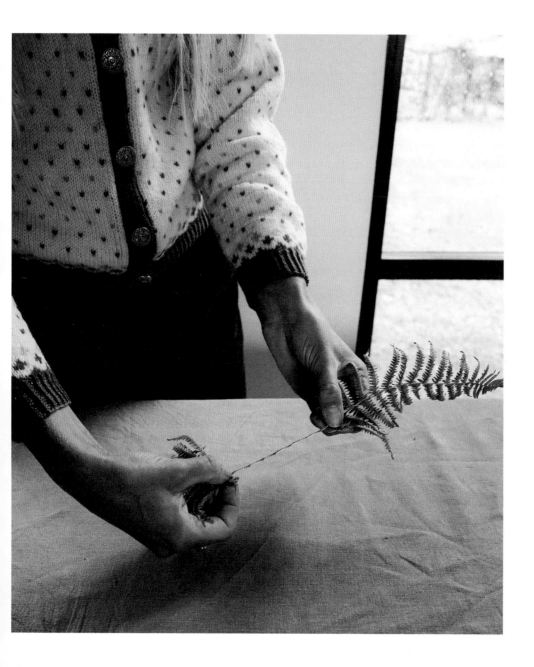

Method

1. It's important for this design that the wreath base you use has plenty of vines twisted together to allow for the stems of the flowers and leaves to be securely inserted into it.

2. Prepare the stems by stripping off any unwanted leaves. This may involve snipping off any lumps along the stems. As you need to carefully feed the stems into the wreath base, it is crucial that they are as smooth as possible to allow for ease of entry.

3. Begin by building up the base layer, carefully inserting stems of foliage at various points around the entire wreath, paying attention to the front, inner circle and outer sides. This wreath is full and abundant, and the base layer will define the shape of the wreath.

4. Next begin to add in the flowers and seedheads, always working in the same direction and ensuring that there is good coverage across the entire wreath.

5. Continue layering and adding in flowers and seedheads, building up a beautiful display and clustering types of flowers together in much the same way as they would grow in the wild.

6. From time to time hang your wreath on a wall and stand back to assess how it looks from a distance and against a flat surface. It's amazing how different they can look when hung up versus laying down on a workbench.

Creating with Nature

We live in a world where it's so easy to source manufactured products to work with. In fact, in many ways it is easier and most definitely faster to hop onto a website and order for next-day delivery than it is to think of an alternative, one that can be found outside. But this is not an environmentally sustainable way of working, and our mindset needs to change.

For the projects in this book I have done some of the hard work for you so you can be making and creating with as little impact on the planet as possible. I've tried to work with materials that are natural, even when they are manufactured (string, for example), so that any project can then be composted when the time comes or – in the case of some of the living designs – replanted in the garden to grow the following year. I've aimed for as little waste as possible when it comes to each project design.

This approach is at the heart of my business and one that I wanted to carry through here as well. Before floral foam, cable ties and plastic-coated wire were available to use, nature provided us with the solutions to our crafting challenges. There is pretty much everything we could need already out there in the natural world: it just takes a little bit of consideration, time and experimentation to find what works.

As with all foraging and offerings from the wild, we need to choose carefully and considerately in order not to strip the land and plants when we are gathering. A little here and there is going to be OK, but please do check your foraging rules and if in doubt, simply don't take.

CREATIVE SOLUTIONS WITH NATURAL MATERIALS

For structure:
Willow branches
Silver birch twigs (the long dangly
    ones work well)
Hazel branches
Vines such as hops, ivy, clematis,
    honeysuckle and wisteria

Moisture retainers:
Moss (gathered responsibly)
Leaves

To secure:
Twine
Raffia
String
Wool string

Vessel structure:
Frog pins
Hard twigs curled up and around
    the vessel

Dried Flower Globe

This dried flower globe was entirely inspired by one of my favourite plants in the garden, smoke bush. Smoke bush has the most incredible blooms, which literally look like smoke billowing from its surface. The bush grows wild in France (and is cultivated elsewhere), where the roadsides are covered in these incredible plants with their ethereal seedheads from midsummer onwards. I knew it would make the perfect base for a flower globe, light and airy but with enough bulk to form the base.

The flowers can be a little tricky to dry and cut at the right time: cut them too early and they will shrivel in the vase, but leave them too late and they will disperse with the wind. Timing is key. I worked with all fresh materials when putting my flower globe together, allowing them to dry in situ and evolve over time. I selected materials that I knew would maintain their structure and form when drying out in this way (versus being hung up to dry), and that gave the flower globe longevity. I also knew that the stems I selected wouldn't wilt and had enough strength to hold their shape well.

This design can also be created using previously dried flowers. Choose a selection of blooms that will complement each other, ensuring that there is a good base of fluffy filler to give your flower globe a full appearance.

Creating the structure for the base took a long time to work out: I knew I needed something that would hold the stems in place and wanted to try to create it entirely out of natural materials. I had the idea that I could use hazel branches and lengths of willow from the garden, but I found them hard to work with and struggled to get them to stay in position. I finally stumbled across wild honeysuckle in my local woodlands, a fallen stem from the high winds, and discovered this to be the best. The vine had just enough tension in it to allow me to wrap the lengths around and create the required ball shape. With these vines I was able to make a nest-like structure that looked beautiful even on its own. If finding vines is too tricky then you can try scrunching up a ball of chicken wire instead.

Gather

~ Vines to create the structure
~ Flowers and foliage: here I have used smoke bush, ammi, alchemilla mollis and sea lavender
~ Length of twine or ribbon to hang the flower globe

Method

1 Begin by shaping the structure of the flower globe. Wind a long stem of honeysuckle around itself, looping the end through and then in and out of the structure to find resistance. There needs to be enough loops and winds within the overall construction so that you can feed the stems of the flowers into them and the stems can be held tightly in place.
2 Once the base structure is complete, loop the ribbon or twine through the top of the globe and hang it up.
3 Now build up a base layer of the main filler flower, in this instance the smoke bush. View the globe from all angles to ensure a good coverage throughout.
4 Next add in interesting stems such as ammi, alchemilla mollis and sea lavender. I like to create waves of these flowers throughout the design, with the delicate white flowers of the ammi looking like stars in the night sky.
5 Spin the globe around on its ribbon to check that it looks good from all angles, and then hang it in its final position.

Botanically
Dyed Ribbons

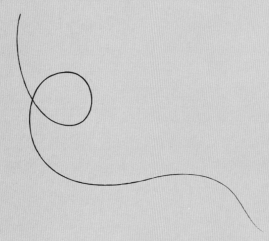

Dyeing fabric using plant materials is one of the most magical projects to undertake. I have only recently started my journey with fabric dyeing and can already feel myself becoming a little obsessed with the alchemy. If you would like to explore the wonders of botanically dyeing fabric further, I have listed some of my favourite creatives who are working in this field at the back of the book for you to explore.

Along with petal printing (see page 100), bundle dyeing is one of the easiest ways to dye fabrics and is a great place to get started as results are guaranteed. I wanted to create rich lengths of ribbon to use in the projects for this book so I selected a soft habotai silk to work with, but bundle dyeing works brilliantly with most fabrics. I don't go into detail here about the preparation methods for dyeing different fabrics, but it's worth reading up on the science behind prepping and mordanting before you get started: there are processes that fabrics need to go through to ensure that the dyes from flowers and plants affix to the materials and last for a longer period of time. I was less concerned about this for these ribbons as I love to see the colours evolve over time, but I wanted to point this out to avoid disappointment for those of you looking to dye fabrics for longevity.

It is enchanting to see the colours that different flowers and plants leave behind. It is not as simple as taking a red rose and assuming that the colour the petals leave behind will be red – it's often the total opposite, and this makes the whole process even more thrilling. This form of dyeing is achievable for all of us, even those who have no access to flowers: avocado and onion skins can produce some wonderful tones (avocado creates a stunning soft pink dye and onion skins give a rich golden colour). So if flowers aren't an option, then know that the kitchen cupboard and fridge can be raided to create beautifully dyed fabrics.

I also find it fascinating that some botanicals which we would think of as being brilliant dyers are actually not. Some of the most vibrant flowers don't actually transpose their colours onto fabric very well at all, and the same goes for some vegetables. Beetroot may stain your clothes and your hands bright red, but when used in bundle dyeing it will fade quickly over time. It's worth doing a bit of research into those plants and flowers that dye well before embarking on a dyeing project; either look online or check out the creatives I list later in this book.

Gather

- ~ Fabric: I sourced an organic silk habotai
- ~ Lots of flower heads, leaves and vegetable skins: here I used cosmos, roses, calendulas, clematis, buddleia, onion skins, avocado skins, fresh turmeric, rose leaves, dahlias and nasturtiums
- ~ Twine
- ~ Saucepan
- ~ Colander or steamer
- ~ Fine spray bottle filled with apple cider vinegar (organic if possible)

Method

1. Lay the fabric out flat on a surface.
2. Spritz the fabric with a mist of the apple cider vinegar until it's saturated.
3. Starting at one end of the fabric, individually lay out petals, vegetable cuttings and leaves. At this point the petals and other pieces can be placed to create patterns on the fabric (I'm far too messy to bother with this but it is an option). The plant materials should not be layered on top of each other but placed alongside, always allowing for a little bit of negative space.
4. Once the first section of the fabric is covered, begin to roll the fabric up with the petals and plant materials in place by tucking in the edge of the end closest to you and rolling as tightly as possible.
5. Because of the length of my fabric, I had to roll and prepare it in sections. Once the first section had been rolled, I pulled the next length of fabric onto the surface, spritzed with the vinegar and layered more petals, flowers and leaves on top.
6. Continue in this way until the whole length of fabric is tightly wound up into a big sausage shape.
7. Working from one end of the bound fabric, roll up until you form a snail shape. Again, roll as tightly as possible as you want the plant material to have plenty of contact with the fabric during the steaming process.
8. Cut a length of twine and wind this around the snail shape to ensure that it is tightly

bound together in all places. Secure with a double knot.

9   Next take your steamer, or saucepan with colander sat on top, and pour in enough hot water to sit below the steamer or colander.

10 Place the bundle of fabric into the steamer or colander, ensuring it's not sitting in contact with the water. Cover with a lid and gently steam on a slow simmer for two hours.

11 Every half an hour or so, turn the bundle of fabric over and ensure that the water is topped up if it begins to look low.

12 After a couple of hours are up, remove the bundle and leave for a day to cool.

13 Once cool, take the fabric outside and open up the bundle, shaking it out to get rid of any petals and other debris. Hang the fabric out to dry out of direct sunlight.

14 Once the fabric has dried, gently iron it on a low heat to remove any wrinkles.

15 Create the ribbons by snipping the fabric at one end to the width you would like your ribbons to be and then simply tearing it down the length.

Meadow Grass Bouquet

My love affair with grasses has been building over the years that I've been growing, gardening and creating with nature. I adore their soft, ethereal qualities and how they can transform a garden with their gentle swaying in the summer months. When we moved to Devon, the first thing we decided to do was to stop mowing the carefully cultivated lawn that we inherited. It was an experiment to see what would appear, and I was amazed at the sheer variety of grasses that flowered that first year, grasses that had been razed to the ground regularly and never given the chance to flourish. It kick-started my obsession and was when I really started to incorporate grasses into my work.

This creative make is a celebration of the often overlooked yet always abundant grasses that can be found in the wild, and in our gardens in cultivated varieties. I wanted to push myself to work with only grasses, to see what beauty they could produce in the form of a bouquet. I adore the end result: there is a lightness to this design that is mesmerising. If I could have my wedding again, I can imagine filling an old barn with just grasses and walking down the aisle with this in my hand.

Incredibly, there are over 10,000 species of grasses in the world, with over 150 to be found in the UK, from rushes and reeds to feathery ornamental grasses. Identifying wild grasses is a real challenge as the differences between species can be so slight that an expert would be needed. I have shared some of my favourite wild grasses and a few of my favourite cultivated grasses on page 136, but the best thing to do is simply take a walk at the height of the summer and see what you can find. The thing with grasses is that they are so often passed over in favour of other exciting materials such as flowers and seedheads, so it takes a little bit of extra looking to notice the good ones. Because they are so readily available and abundant, for the most part we can feel confident in foraging for stems without causing any damage. The best time to pick grasses is in the summer, when they are still in the green and before they have gone on to set seed. Picking them at this point means the stem and flower head will remain intact.

I have used a selection of soft, floaty grasses in the mix here, which give the bouquet a lovely openness, alongside more structured stems that punctuate the cloud-like structure and add interest and intrigue.

WILD GRASSES

Red fescue
Yorkshire fog
Creeping bent
Meadow foxtail
Cock's-foot
Crested dog's-tail

ANNUAL AND PERENNIAL GRASSES

Stipa: all of them, they look stunning dotted
    around a flower bed
Canary grass
Briza media (also maxia, but media is my favourite)
Fibre optic grass
Miscanthus
Tufted hair grass 'Goldtau'
Fountain grass 'Red head' and 'Fairy tails'

Gather

~ Stems of grasses, picked fresh or from
  the drying rack. You will need many
  more than you think in order to achieve
  a voluminous bouquet
~ Natural twine
~ Snips
~ Botanically dyed ribbons (see page 128)

Method

1. I find when creating bouquets, that it's best to build a frame with some sturdy stems first and the same applies when creating this wild grass bouquet. Take three strong stems of grass and place them in a triangle shape – hold them together with the forefinger and thumb. This gathering of stems becomes the start of the bouquet.

2. Within this frame, begin to weave in the lighter, fluffier, more delicate stems of grasses. Gently push the stems down from the middle of the bouquet whilst also spiralling out from the outside of the bouquet.

3. Once the main frame and surrounds are full enough, I then place in a structural grass such as cockfoot, which provides a little bit of interest and serves to break up the visuals of the bouquet.

4. Pay close attention to the shape of the bottom stems of your bouquet, we are aiming for a spiralled shape, mirroring the outwards movement of the main bouquet. Secure the stems of the bouquet together with string tied in a bow.

5. Neaten up the ends of the bouquet by trimming down the stems until they are all cut to the same length. Once this has been done the bouquet should be able to stand upright on its own.

6. I chose to wrap a length of botanically dyed ribbon around the string to finish off.

Practising Creativity

In the early days of my creative journey, long before it became my profession, I would regularly, often daily, practise creativity. Without consciously setting an intention, I felt a deep-rooted urge to do so. During moments when my baby slept, I would immerse myself in making small arrangements, experimenting with compositions and capturing them through the lens of a camera. I became consumed by this process, with friends and family affectionately dubbing my endeavours as 'faffing with flowers'. Rather than buying blooms, I chose to forage and gather from the garden and surrounding landscapes, fostering a connection with the seasons. This intimate relationship with nature continues to influence my artistic style and approach to this day.

Engaging in creative practices, particularly with nature, has the remarkable ability to cultivate peace and joy. I've witnessed this firsthand through my workshops, where guests will fall into a deep sense of calm and concentration during the workshop, often engaging in emotional and personal conversations as the act of working with their hands and nature's beauty softens them.

Now that my creative pursuits have become my job, it has become harder to find the time to create for creativity's sake. With clients' needs to be met and teaching becoming a huge part of my work, time to play became more and more limited, and I was instead creating on demand. Recently, I've made a conscious effort to reintegrate these practices into my daily life, starting with small, manageable steps to encourage the habit to return. It's essential not to let the pressure of any intention overwhelm us; if we miss a day or even a week, it's okay. The journey of creativity is fluid and forgiving, and sometimes a moment's respite can be just as nourishing as creative output. Above all, it's important to be kind to ourselves as we navigate this ongoing journey of self-expression and growth. Some days may flow effortlessly, while others may feel frustrating and stagnant: each experience is valuable and worthy of acknowledgment.

Finding the time

Depending on your personality and preferences, you might choose to carve out a dedicated time each day for your creative pursuits, or, like me, you could opt for a more spontaneous approach, weaving creative moments throughout your day. I'm often in my garden or working inside on the computer, and it's these tasks that I chose to intersperse with moments of creativity. Whether it's sowing seeds in the greenhouse, responding to emails or tending to seedlings, these creative micro-moments offer a much-needed break from the demands of daily life and allow me to reset and refocus. Over time, these creative interludes become ingrained habits, seamlessly woven into the fabric of my daily routine. I've even taken this practice away with me, whether it's collecting shells on the beach or gathering wildflowers while camping. By embracing creativity in everyday moments, we enrich our lives and nourish our souls, no matter where we are.

The following are two ways in which I introduce a little bit of creativity into my life each day:

Creating in miniature

The beauty of creating teeny-tiny versions of projects is that they take very little time and they encourage us to really focus in on the materials we are using. When working with the smallest of stems, it is impossible to rush, slow is the only way to go. I began this practice by creating a tiny flower arrangement in a small bud vase whenever I could find a moment. Even if all I could see when I stepped outside was a blade of grass and a daisy, I would still spend a few moments arranging those in my chosen vessel. This is simple and achievable, and all the while allows us to flex our creative muscles and keep noticing.

Photography

I find that one of the easiest ways of spending a bit of time in my creative mindset is through photography. It takes seconds to pick up my phone or camera and capture an image of something that has caught my eye or inspired me. This is such an interesting form of creativity, as it often helps me to see things in a completely different way, challenging preconceived ideas and thoughts that I may have had.

Retreating

5

Embracing winter has been a journey for me, one that has brought a deeper appreciation for the season and its significance.

It's a time when nature slows down, conserving energy and preparing for renewal in the spring. And just as nature adapts to the changing seasons, so too must we find ways to nurture ourselves during the darker months.

Leaving behind the confines of an office and immersing myself in the natural world has been transformative. Instead of rushing through the cold darkness from car to door, I now find solace in the crisp air and the quiet beauty of winter landscapes. While stark bare branches and muddy ground may seem bleak at first glance, there is a quiet resilience to be found in the simplicity of winter's palette.

Rather than dwelling on the 'dreariness' of winter, I've learned to find peace and nourishment in its rituals and rhythms. From cosy nights by the fire to brisk walks on a clear, frosty morning, there is a sense of purpose and renewal that underlies the season's challenges. Nature is for the most part dormant during winter; it is resting, shielding itself from the worst of the weather and preparing for a new season. I have tried to reflect the acts of nature in the way that I approach winter: while the modern world encourages us to be always switched on and striving for more and better, we also need time to rest. Winter is that time for me. Work slows down in January and February, as do my energy levels. I focus on time with my family, nesting and hibernating, with stews on the hob and candlelight filling the living spaces. It is a quiet time, of reflection and introspection, a season to slow down and appreciate the simple things.

Racing against time, I plant out as many bulbs as I can in December: this is an act of self-care, planning ahead for when spring arrives. I'm looking for sunshine-yellow joy in the bulbs I select as I dig holes for hundreds of narcissi to flood my garden with a sea of gold and ivory for the whole of spring. If there is one thing I urge you to do in midwinter, it's to plant some bulbs, even if only for an indoor garden or a pot by your front door. These blooms are life-giving after the dreariness of the darker days.

Beauty in chaos

Living in the countryside has heightened my awareness of the weather's impact, especially during storms. The thick mud and stark landscapes can sometimes feel overwhelming, and I find myself despairing at the mess outside. Yet, as my husband Ed often reminds me, nature's disorder holds its own beauty.

Amid the chaos of fallen leaves and tangled branches, there is life teeming beneath the surface. Insects seek shelter among the seedheads and leaf mulch, finding refuge in the very messiness that initially dismayed me. I've learned to reframe my perspective, finding solace in the hidden beauty of nature's disarray.

The arrival of the first flowers of the season brings a sense of wonder and gratitude. Snowdrops emerge from the frigid earth with remarkable strength, pushing through leaves and debris as they make their way towards the light. Each year I'm astounded by their tenacity as they blanket the banks and verges in swathes of delicate white blooms.

Following closely behind the snowdrops are camellias and hellebores, adding splashes of colour to the winter landscape. I find myself marvelling at their ability to flourish in such harsh conditions. It's a reminder of nature's resilience, and I'm deeply grateful for their presence. Sometime in January I pick my first stems for the house and fill teeny-tiny bud vases with a smattering of stems to sit on my desk and bedside table.

Most of the winter here in the West Country is spent sheltering from the storms, with our garden whipped into a frenzy by the westerlies that continue to push through on the ever-powerful jet stream. However, we do from time-to-time experience periods of crisp, clear days where the sky is cornflower blue and the garden is coated with a light sprinkling of frost. These are my favourite days, yanked out of bed by the lightness in the air after so many mornings of fog and grey, standing in the garden in my pyjamas, camera in hand to capture the intricate frosty artworks glistening on seedheads and grasses. The garden is transformed into a winter wonderland, so pretty and ethereal, a stolen moment in time.

Endings and new beginnings

When the first crocus and winter aconite make their appearance, I greet them with glee, revelling in their delicate blooms against the backdrop of winter's grasp. This season encourages me to pay attention to the smallest shifts, to home in on the beauty of nature even in its dormant state. By immersing myself in these details, I stay grounded in the present moment, fully embracing the season for all its wonders without longing for what lies ahead.

I try as much as possible to spend time outside every day, knowing that this is what helps me fight against the melancholy of winter. Cycles to the sea for a very quick dip are fierce and painful, and I fall in the front door to nestle against the woodburner and feel some heat back in my body. Mulching the garden keeps my hands busy and my body warm as I cover all my beds with a thick layer of mulch, feeding the soil after a long year of hard work and at the same time providing a barrier against weeds. Up and down the garden I trundle with my wheelbarrow, the beds a satisfying neat and tidy space when all covered up with their winter coat – the plants will thank me next year for nourishing the soil so deeply. I try my hardest to not yearn for spring, to go slowly and enjoy the space and time that winter affords: it won't be long before spring returns and the cycle begins once more.

Honesty Wreath

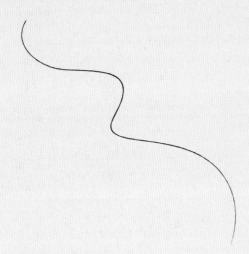

Sometimes simple is best, and this wreath is a perfect example of just that. Created using my absolute favourite all-season seedpod, honesty, it couldn't be easier to piece together this beauty. Honesty, when peeled, provides shimmering joy: in the depths of winter when the world outside can feel dull and unwelcoming, it serves to lift our spirits and reminds us how magical nature is. These wreaths are one of the most popular items in my shop at Christmas. Hung on front doors or in the home, they are a statement piece that can be reused year after year to bring sparkle inside.

Honesty grows freely in hedgerows in the UK (and is cultivated in temperate zones around the world), and can be spied from late summer onwards, recognisable by its silvery seed pods – which are actually the inside of the pod once the outer casing has been removed by hand or by the elements. Honesty is a biannual, meaning the seeds need to be sown in early summer to flower and set seed the following year. They have deep taproots so are tricky to transplant when grown as seedlings, and in my garden I find they prefer to grow along the edges, nestled among the wildflowers and brambles, rather than in the growing spaces.

It took me a good few years to realise that honesty benefits from being picked and dried earlier in the season than you would anticipate: if you wait until nature has done her thing and removed the outer casing of seedpods for you, you will find that this is too late. The optimal time for picking honesty is when the seedpods have turned leathery to touch and rattle when you shake the branches, and when you feel or see the developed seeds behind the leathery outer casing. The seedpods themselves will still at this point have retained much of their colour (rather than fading to a golden hue), and picking them now ensures that the structure of the plant remains intact, making peeling the seedpods much easier.

The process of revealing that magical inner structure is mesmerising. I spend many an evening sitting in front of the fire during winter, diligently stripping my honesty of its outer clothes. When fully dried, carefully peel back either side of the seedpod using a fingernail to hook under the seedpod edge at either the top or the bottom. If they are dried and at a good stage, then this outer casing should easily come away to reveal the incredible silvery insides. Remember to save all the seeds that will be dispersed as you strip the honesty of their outer shells to scatter in your garden or in the hedgerows next year.

Gather

~ Moss wreath base
~ Good armful of peeled honesty

Method

1 Create your moss wreath by wrapping layers of moss around your vine wreath base. Secure the moss in place with a length of twine, or if you prefer wire.
2 Working with honesty that has already had its outer casing removed, cut down the stems to shorter lengths, ensuring that you leave enough stem to poke into the moss wreath.
3 Starting anywhere on the wreath base, carefully insert the honesty stems, always working in the same direction.
4 Focus on ensuring that the front, inner circle and outer edges are as full as can be while allowing each branch its own space to breath. Overcrowding the wreath can lessen the beauty of the seedpods by making it look cluttered and compacted.
5 Continue until the entire wreath is covered in the honesty seedpods.
6 Hang on your front door or inside to enjoy throughout winter.

Flower Garlands

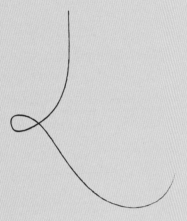

Strawflowers are my absolute favourite dried flowers, both for their longevity and for the pure, unadulterated joy they bring. Their radiant faces brighten any day or dark corner, and I greet their return each year with such happiness. They are also one of the best dried flowers to work with because they maintain their colour for so long and are structurally very sturdy. This makes them perfect for crafting, whether you're including them in wreaths or making garlands such as these.

In the past it was common to cut strawflowers to dry and then wire their heads in place. This was partly to stop the heads from flopping, which can often happen, but also because they are prone to falling off their stems. I don't do this as I embrace their movement and tend not to use unnecessary wire in my work, but that does mean that I often end up with lots of loose heads as they ping off when I'm working. This creative make is the perfect way to use up any spare flower heads left over from other projects.

Growing strawflowers is super easy too. They are a hardy annual, which means they can withstand colder temperatures, and for that reason I have begun to sow mine in autumn and then overwinter them in the greenhouse as seedlings before planting out in early spring. This gives me a good crop of early flowers in June. To pick strawflowers for drying, allow the first few main flowers to open fully to show their centres and let the stems harden (no floppiness!) Cut the first stem down by a quarter or so, removing the main flower head and any slightly open buds that are beginning to flower just below the main flower; any side shoots will go on to bring more flowers later in the summer. Strawflowers usually continue to open a little once dried, so bear this in mind when cutting. Simply hang out to dry following the guide on page 22.

These strawflower garlands are one of the simplest, most effective ways to decorate your home in winter. While these garlands have been woven together with dried flowers, they can also be created with fresh flowers in summer – marigolds and calendula would work beautifully and will dry while hanging, making an ever-evolving display for your home in the summer months.

Dried garlands look stunning hung from a mantelpiece at Christmas or strung from the corners of a dark space in the house. They can be used to decorate Christmas trees for extra festive cheer, weaving them in and out of the dense evergreen branches to nestle among vintage baubles, the soft glow from fairy lights helping them to sparkle. They will last a long time, so can be packaged up and stored in a cardboard box wrapped in tissue paper for the following year.

Gather

- ~ Strawflower heads
- ~ Twine: I have selected a twine with gold thread running through it for festive shimmer, but you could use any thread or twine
- ~ A large needle: one used for darning seems to be best

Method

1. Cut a length of thread or twine and thread it onto the needle. I have been working in 200 cm (80 in) lengths, which feels like a good amount to string among the branches of a Christmas tree or across the ceiling or mantelpiece. Tie a loop at the end of the thread.

2. With the flower heads all facing in the same direction, carefully pierce the head of each flower from the base through the centre. I find it easier to go this way as there is more resistance to press into when pushing the needle through. Once the needle has passed, carefully pull it and the thread all the way through, pulling the flower head down to the bottom of the thread.

3. Continue threading the flower heads onto the thread, spacing them about 2.5 cm (1 in) or so apart until you have filled the entire length of thread.

4. Once you have reached the end of the thread make a small loop from which to hang the garland.

Nature's Finest
Chandelier

Christmas is my most treasured time of year. The run-up can be one of the most stressful times, as I work hard to get all my wreaths out the door and spend hours teaching winter wreath workshops, but this busyness just serves to build excitement for all that is to come. Once the orders have been made and shipped I can finally close the door to my studio and ease myself into the calm of the festive period, where long, lazy days are spent with family and friends. It's a chance to relax and take stock of all that the year has delivered.

One gift that I always give myself at this time of year is the space and time to decorate the house. It's the only time that I'm allowed free rein to bring flowers and seedheads into the house in such abundance, and I relish this moment. It's been a long-standing tradition of mine to decorate our table for dinner on Christmas day, and filling the space with shimmering seedheads and glowing candles brings me so much joy – perhaps even more than eating the traditional meal.

The beauty of decorating in the depths of winter is that the simplest of materials can transform a space into something incredible. A statuesque branch placed in the corner of a room and decorated with delicate copper fairy lights can be as enchanting as the Christmas tree itself, it's all about how to bring some sparkle to the home. With so many hours of darkness here in the UK (we have only 7–8 days of sunlight in the depths of winter) we have to make our own light and magic.

A FEW OF MY FAVOURITE
SEEDHEADS FOR WINTER
DECORATIONS

Clematis, both wild and cultivated
Honesty
Catananche, a perennial
  cornflower
Stipa grasses
Briza media

Gather

- ~ Branch: I chose one from our old beech
  tree with leaves and fruit casings intact
- ~ Honesty seedpods
- ~ Thin gauge wire
- ~ Clematis seedheads
- ~ Brass leaves

Method

1   Working with small stems of peeled honesty,
    attach individual stems to the open ends of the
    branch using strips of the thin gauge wire.

2   Fill the branch with as many honesty seedpods
    as possible, ensuring there is a good balance
    and plenty of negative space. Consider if the
    branch is to be viewed from all sides and make
    sure the placing of the honesty reflects this.

3   Once the branch has been filled, hang it in
    position using a length of string or wire on each
    side. Temporary command hooks can be used
    to avoid damaging walls if preferred.

4   Lay the table with crockery and cutlery and
    then cluster candles of various lengths and
    sizes. I adore beeswax candles for their scent
    and simplicity.

5   In among the candles and tableware, dot
    around vessels or frog pins with clematis
    seedheads positioned inside. It's nice to vary
    the lengths of seedheads for interest and to
    give a more organic feel to the visuals.

6   Finally, string the brass leaves from the
    overhanging branch. The brass leaves are
    a cute addition to the design, although by
    no means essential, and will sway softly in
    the heat of the candles once they are lit.

Finding Flow

Creativity is not something that can easily be produced on demand. Our minds are busy bees, flitting from one thing to another, finding distractions along the way and sometimes actually being obstructive. Negative thoughts can find their way in, disrupting our focus and ability to drop into a creative state. This can be frustrating and often debilitating.

I have written a lot about the importance of focusing on the process rather than the end result, and there is a reason for suggesting this. By zoning in on the journey rather than what we are trying to achieve, we can free our minds of the anxiety and stresses of whether we are going to meet our own or others' expectations. Working creatively with nature helps in many ways to free us from our noisy mind. Because there are no rules or rights and wrongs, it's a freeing way to spend time, allowing us to leave anxieties at the door.

The state of flow, or being 'in the zone', is achieved when we are entirely focused on one task or activity, the consequence being that we have little to no other thoughts. We lose track of time and can't be distracted by the outside world, be it noises, other people or changes in temperature. It is the very best state in which to create and where I strive to be most days but often don't achieve. Being in flow state allows us to expand our experiences and practise our skills at a deeper level, and can also help to support and enhance our productivity.

Flow state can be achieved and supported with a few nudges:

~ Make sure the task you are working on is challenging enough; it should be difficult enough to capture your focus as your brain works hard to complete it, but not so difficult that it becomes frustrating. You may find it tough to achieve flow when creating a project from this book for the first time, but once you've practised a few times, it will come. For example, I tend to find flow easily when creating wreaths and bouquets, both of which I am well practised at but which still need thought to consider textures and colours to put them together.
~ Flow states generally occur during long activities rather than shorter ones. I often find myself in flow at my weekly pottery classes, head down and hands in clay.
~ Try to minimise outside distractions: this could look like leaving your phone in another room, putting on headphones with focus music playing or ensuring that urgent tasks are tackled before you set about beginning a project.

The Bones of Winter Wreath

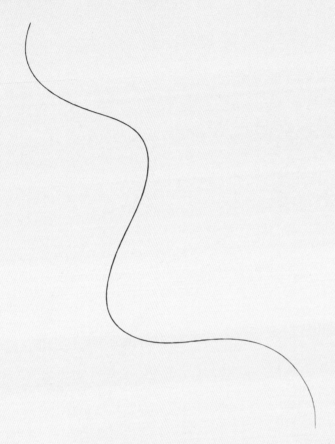

Winter can feel desolate and draining at times. It can be hard to see the beauty in among the mud and inclement weather, but it is there – we just need to look a little closer and work a little harder to find it. Lichen-covered branches and ripened red rosehips are two of my favourite things at this time of year. My focus shifts to the structural elements in the garden, hedgerows and woodlands, and it's less about flowers and obvious prettiness and more about the hidden beauty.

My regular walks in the woods and surroundings help to keep me connected to nature during this season. It's all too easy to spend time indoors during the darker winter months and avoid the cold and rain, but this can lead to us disconnecting from the natural world and stops us from truly appreciating the beauty of winter. I love the bracing walks as much as I love returning home to a warm house to hunker down by the fire and eat comforting stews and crumbles. Time outside makes the time spent inside so much more special and appreciated.

This wreath is really simple and delicate, and has been pieced together using just a very few stems of the best of mid-winter. Waving grasses, faded from the rain and the wind, are combined with fluffy seedheads. A flash of red from the rosehips lifts the design and brings interest to the eye, while the movement of the grasses is replicated in the twigs that shoot off to the side. The wreath embodies a sense of movement and flow.

Gather

- ~ Vines for the wreath base: because these will be exposed, seek out vines with a bit of interest to them, such as wild honeysuckle or hop vines
- ~ Sticks and grasses that have a feel of flow and beauty
- ~ Interesting seedheads and botanicals: here I have used rosehips and clematis seedheads
- ~ Wire
- ~ Twine
- ~ Velvet ribbon

Method

1　Wind the vines into a circular shape, twisting the ends inwards to secure them in place. Because a large section of the wreath base will be visible, aim for an organic, free approach to the shape of the wreath base – lots of loops and curls are ideal.

2　Working with a few stems at a time, attach one or two to the base of the wreath using thin strips of wire to wrap the stems onto the base. The first few stems should face upwards and outwards.

3　Continue to add in stems a few at a time, gradually working around the wreath base. The stems should be long and free-flowing, so attach them at the lower end of the stems to allow the grasses and twigs to flow outwards and not be restricted.

4　Now, starting at the opposite side of the wreath and working in the opposite direction to before, select a few stems that will mirror the upper part of the wreath and attach those to the base.

5　Build up the bottom of the wreath gradually until the ends meet the ends of the top section.

6　Wrap the ribbon around the central point of the wreath where the ends of both sections meet, and tie in a beautiful bow, leaving long ends of the velvet to hang down.

Ethereal Swag

The word 'swag' has many meanings in the English language. In this instance, it simply means 'to hang down in a decorative way'. A swag is a collection of branches and stems, gathered together in a way that allows them to drape beautifully when in their chosen position. I fell in love with swags as an alternative to wreaths a few years ago, as a result of making so many wreaths for clients at Christmas that I simply could not face making my own. So a swag it was.

Swags look simple to make but actually take some consideration to get just right. I find that the fewer the ingredients, the better the swag. There is real beauty in simplicity and in allowing each stem its own space to be seen.

Featured in this swag is one of my all-time favourite ingredients to use during the autumn and winter: wild clematis seedheads – also known as old man's beard. Wild clematis grows rampantly among the hedgerows in the UK and is easily recognisable from late summer onwards, when the delicate white flowers begin to shift to sparkly green seedheads. This change happens around early autumn time and signals the point at which the clematis seedheads should be cut.

I harvest armfuls of the seedheads and bring them inside the studio to 'ripen' in the warmth. Cutting them at this stage allows for the very delicate seeds to puff out and fluff up without being exposed to the elements, which can strip the seeds from the main body of the plant and scatter them far and wide. Wild clematis can also discolour if left on the stem through into late autumn, with the weather turning them a murky colour over time.

This swag is created using just two ingredients, both of which are already dried. Alternatively, you can gather evergreens from the forest and use those as the base for your swag, dotting in the occasional strawflower or stem of honesty to brighten up the greens. Hung on the front door, it will last for the whole festive period.

Gather

~ Selection of stems: here I have used honesty and clematis
~ Twine
~ Ribbon

Method

1 Begin by gathering your stems into a bunch. The swag will be sitting against a flat wall or door, so ensure that the back of the swag is a flat as possible, avoiding any stems that would encourage it to sit lopsided or away from the wall.

2 In terms of shape, I tend to aim for a long, thin shape that gathers to a tip at the end. To achieve this, select the best honesty stem that will allow you to define the shape of the final piece.

3 Around this stem, nestle in lengths of wild clematis seedheads, ensuring that the pearly discs of the honesty have space to shine through.

4 Tie off the ends with a length of twine to secure them.

5 Trim the ends of the stems so they are all in a neat line.

6 Finish with a luxurious bow – I am a big fan of velvet ribbons at this time of year.

Index

Suppliers and Further Reading

HOBBYCRAFT
hobbycraft.co.uk (also in the US)
For all your wire, twine and scissor needs

DRIED FLOWER SUPPLIERS
(beyond local flower farmers)
lsfwholesale.co.uk
barnflorist.co.uk

BULBS AND POTTED PLANTS
crocus.co.uk
farmergracy.co.uk

THREAD AND WOOL
oxfordweavingstudio.com

SILKS FOR RIBBON DYEING
organicsilks.co.uk

BRASS LEAVES TO DECORATE WINTER DISPLAYS
alba-jewellery.co.uk

VELVET RIBBONS
floristrywarehouse.com

FURTHER READING AND EXPLORATION

Sources for locating flower farms and florists:
UK
flowersfromthefarm.co.uk

USA
slowflowers.com/listing

floretflowers.com/directory

localflowers.org

Fabric dyeing expert Babs Behan:
botanicalinks.com
And her book *Botanical Dyes*

To delve into the world of Japanese seasons and culture seek out Beth Kempton and her books: *Wabi Sabi* and *Kokoro*

Still: The Art of Noticing by Mary Jo Hoffman is a beautiful book which surveys the natural world and celebrates noticing all that surrounds us

About the Author

Founder of Botanical Tales, Bex Partridge is a floral artist specialising in dried flowers whose work is continually inspired by nature and the ebb and flow of the seasons. Bex is the author of two books, *Everlastings* and *Flowers Forever*, both diving into the ethereal world of dried flowers. Bex creates installations and art for people's homes and spaces, as well as teaching others the art of creating with flowers as the medium. She shares advice and inspiration through her social media channels, newsletter and substack.

Acknowledgements

The piecing together of this book has felt as though I have come full circle. Taking a step back to remind myself of how I found myself in this flowery world has been cathartic and invigorating. I have so enjoyed spending time dreaming up projects and revisiting some from back when Botanical Tales was a seed of a dream. I still find it mind bogglingly bonkers that I get to do this for my day job, each and every day, it is truly a dream come true.

The biggest thanks to my Quadrille team, for Kajal who saw the potential in a book that took a little while to tease out, to Chelsea for impeccable management – keeping everyone on track to deliver it on time despite a shortened deadline. For this book I was lucky enough to work with two photographers, to ensure we captured every little seasonal change on time! So, to Laura for agreeing to come down and spend another week with me on the hill, snapping thousands of photos in the way only she knows how to do, incredible beauty as always. And to Alice, who agreed to the project after some gentle persuasion, the images are beautiful and I am so grateful for all the effort you put into making the book so very special.

To Rose, the biggest thank you for your input into the design and aesthetics of the book in those oh so important, very early stages, your incredible eye for detail set me on the right path to create a book that feels exactly right for me and my work, I'm so grateful!

A few thank yous to all those wonderful friends and neighbours who supported me. To Andy for allowing me to roam free in his beautiful wildflower field, cutting buttercups for projects and for drying, I am so grateful. And to Alice and Michelle for allowing me to raid their shop, kitchens and homes for all the best props – you'll see them scattered throughout the pages and they make so many of the photos infinitely better. Zoe, thank you for allowing me the use of your magical barn to capture the winter shots.

To my boys, Henry and Arlo, who have for the first time understood what writing a book means. Who have been inquisitive, supportive and proud of the process, I love you with all my heart, to the moon and back.

And finally to Ed. There aren't really enough words to say what I want to. But just the biggest thanks for everything; building my new studio whilst I focused on this book was an incredible task and one that you took on so willingly and kindly. You fully deserve to have your photo in the book (finally!).

Quadrille, Penguin Random House UK, One Embassy Gardens, 8 Viaduct Gardens, London SW11 7BW

Quadrille Publishing Limited is part of the Penguin Random House group of companies whose addresses can be found at global.penguinrandomhouse.com

In accordance with Article 4(3) of the DSM Directive 2019/790, Penguin Random House expressly reserves this work from the text and data mining exception.

Published by Quadrille in 2025

www.penguin.co.uk

A CIP catalogue record for this book is available from the British Library
ISBN 9781784887810

10 9 8 7 6 5 4 3 2 1

Publishing Director: Kajal Mistry
Acting Publishing Director: Judith Hannam
Managing Editor: Chelsea Edwards
Designer: Vanessa Masci
Photographers: Laura Edwards and Alice Tatham
Copeditor: Gaynor Sermon
Proofreader: Marie Clayton
Indexer: Helen Snaith
Senior Production Controller: Martina Georgieva

Colour reproduction by p2d
Printed in China by C&C Offset Printing Co. , Ltd.

The authorised representative in the EEA is Penguin Random House Ireland, Morrison Chambers, 32 Nassau Street, Dublin D02 YH68.

Penguin Random House is committed to a sustainable future for our business, our readers and our planet. This book is made from Forest Stewardship Council® certified paper.